Cambridge Elements

Elements in the Renaissance
· edited by
John Henderson
Birkbeck, University of London, and Wolfson College, University of Cambridge
Jonathan K. Nelson
Syracuse University Florence, and Kennedy School, Harvard University

CINDERELLA'S GLASS SLIPPER

Towards a Cultural History of Renaissance Materialities

Genevieve Warwick
University of Edinburgh

CAMBRIDGE
UNIVERSITY PRESS

Shaftesbury Road, Cambridge CB2 8EA, United Kingdom

One Liberty Plaza, 20th Floor, New York, NY 10006, USA

477 Williamstown Road, Port Melbourne, VIC 3207, Australia

314–321, 3rd Floor, Plot 3, Splendor Forum, Jasola District Centre, New Delhi – 110025, India

103 Penang Road, #05–06/07, Visioncrest Commercial, Singapore 238467

Cambridge University Press is part of Cambridge University Press & Assessment, a department of the University of Cambridge.

We share the University's mission to contribute to society through the pursuit of education, learning and research at the highest international levels of excellence.

www.cambridge.org
Information on this title: www.cambridge.org/9781009263986

DOI: 10.1017/9781009263948

First published 2022

A catalogue record for this publication is available from the British Library.

ISBN 978-1-009-26398-6 Paperback
ISSN 2631-9101 (online)
ISSN 2631-9098 (print)

Cinderella's Glass Slipper

Towards a Cultural History of Renaissance Materialities

Elements in the Renaissance

DOI: 10.1017/9781009263948
First published online: October 2022

Genevieve Warwick
University of Edinburgh

Author for correspondence: Genevieve Warwick, g.warwick@gmail.com

Abstract: *Cinderella's Glass Slipper* studies Renaissance material cultures through the literary prism of fairy-tale objects. The literary fairy tale first arose in Renaissance Venice, originating from oral storytelling traditions that would later become the *Arabian Nights*, and subsequently in the Parisian salons of Louis XIV. Largely written by, for, and in the name of women, these literary fairy tales took a lightly comic view of life's vicissitudes, especially female fortune in marriage. Connecting literary representations of bridal goods – dress, jewellery, carriages, toiletries, banqueting, and confectionary – to the craft histories of their making, this Element offers a newly contextualised socio-economic account of Renaissance luxe, from architectural interiors to sartorial fashioning and design. By coupling Renaissance luxury wares with their fairy-tale representation, it locates the recherché materialities of bridal goods – gold, silver, diamonds, and silk – within expanding colonialist markets of a newly global early modern economy in the age of discovery.

This Element also has a video abstract: www.cambridge.org/warwick

Keywords: Renaissance, materialities, fairy tales, decorative arts, dress

ISBNs: 9781009263986 (PB), 9781009263948 (OC)
ISSNs: 2631-9101 (online), 2631-9098 (print)

Contents

1 Introduction   1

2 The Renaissance Fairy Tale   2

3 Luxury Materialities   36

4 Fairy-Tale Objects   49

   References   91

1 Introduction

In the emblematic fairy tales of Sleeping Beauty and Cinderella, the paradigmatic objects of female destiny were specifically those of textile and dress: a spindle, a jewelled gown, and most quixotic of all, a dancing slipper made of glass. From diffuse folkloric origin, the Renaissance rise of the literary fairy tale touched on princely and mercantile misadventures and triumphs, and above all female fortune in marriage, in which magical nuptial artefacts were often key to the narrative turn. First appearing in Renaissance Venice with a further efflorescence in the Parisian *salons* of Louis XIV, it was chiefly authored by, for, and in the name of women. Characterised by enchanted bridal objects of precious materials, its magical objects are couched within a veiled social history of their manufacture. Addressing the study of Renaissance artisanal cultures through the prism of fairy-tale objects and their counterpart in the material artefacts of marriage custom, this Element brings together figurative representations of luxury goods with the craft histories of their making. The sections in turn examine Renaissance fairy-tale objects as literary fictions, luxury goods, and economic commodities. Through an extended discussion of each literary object, the volume draws on a wealth of related Renaissance artisanal histories surrounding luxury artefacts.

Unfolding from Indo-Persian oral storytelling traditions that would subsequently become the *Arabian Nights*, the fairy tale arrived in Renaissance Venice along with the Serenissima's rich Levantine trade in luxury goods, including manuscripts and books. With a scattered appearance across the Italian courts connected with the East, its definitive literary form emerged in *siècle d'or* Paris. The nineteenth century saw the fullest flowering of the fairy tale, notably in the celebrated anthologies by the Brothers Grimm and Hans Christian Andersen. But it was in the seventeenth-century Parisian *salons* that it first gained its soubriquet of 'fairy tale'. In the writings of the renowned *salonnière,* Marie-Catherine le Jumel de Barneville, Baroness d'Aulnoy, the genre took on its definitive title. The detail of Cinderella's glass slipper was also a literary fiction first coined by another *salon* author of d'Aulnoy's *équipe*, Charles Perrault. Administrator for Louis XIV's interior decoration of the French royal palaces, and of the French Manufactories in luxury goods that furnished them, Perrault worked at the fulcrum of French *luxe*. Thus, the sections of this Element proceed along a chronological geography that moves from sixteenth-century Venice to Perrault's Paris, alongside their respective thematic considerations of fairy-tale objects as fictional, precious, and economic goods.

Attending to Max Lüthi and Lucien Febvre's injunction to bring together the disciplines of art history with the sociological study of folklore, this Element twines material culture with the fictive artefacts of its literary representation. It understands the luxury artefact as a particularly dense site of socio-cultural relations embodied within the commodity form, through which it adopts its 'fairy-tale' aspect. Recourse to a burgeoning art-historical scholarship on materialities, here understood as the social properties of things, frames the cultural value attributed to objects defined as 'luxury' or 'precious'. The fairy-tale artefact is above all a materiality of light: of sparkle, lustre, and gleam, a cosmic reflection of the sun, stars and moon also embodied in the auratic perception of royalty. With attention to the telling detail – in this instance, the fictive glass slipper of Cinderella's ballroom dress – the analysis draws on those scholarly literatures arising from the semiotic analysis of words and things at the crossroads of art history, anthropology, historical and literary studies. Through a prismatic enquiry, it prizes open an historical understanding of the 'magic' of things. Their 'enchanted' production was, on the one hand, of folkloric derivation; and on the other hand, tied to Renaissance humanist cultures of alchemical enquiry, bound to the quest for the philosopher's stone. While fairy-tale objects of luxury consumption cannot, in themselves, usefully be reduced to social commentary yet they are suffused with its figurative representation. The artefacts of bridal ritual, constituted within a fairy-tale cast, effected the social transformation of women into marriage. Thus, within the glass slipper's emblematic configuration lies the conceptual 'cloth' of the early modern commodity form. Cinderella's bewitched dress, jewels, and carriage are precious objects, even as the social histories of their production and consumption are riveted with the complexities of economic colonialisms, gender and class. The gossamer impossibility of the fairy-tale object, situated precisely at the threshold of material culture and literary fiction, suggests, however lightly, its social face.[1]

2 The Renaissance Fairy Tale

The earliest fairy tales to appear in print are generally attributed to the pseudonymic Straparola (meaning storyteller), whose collections of short stories published in Venice in the early 1550s included both fables and novellas accompanied by riddles, jokes, and songs. Like Giovanni Boccaccio's *Decameron*, Straparola's *Pleasant Nights* unfolds within a framing text of lightly fictionalised evening entertainments composed of music, dancing, feasting, and stories. Apparently set at the villa of Lucrezia Sforza-Gonzaga on the Venetian island of Murano, the *Pleasant Nights* mirrors the Boccaccesque genre in weaving together its composite fictions of social and narrative place. Over the

---

[1] Febvre, 2009; Lüthi, 1982; Arasse, 1992; Gell, 1992; Warburg, 1999; Brown, 2004.

course of thirteen nights of a carnival season, Lucrezia's guests, comprising both Venetian beauties and celebrated literati such as Pietro Bembo, entertained the company with comedic tales of folklore and fairy-tale fiction. Many are variations on well-known tales from Boccaccio, others derive from the oral sources that would come to form the *Arabian Nights*, surely the source of Straparola's title. Some blend proverbial elements of a Rabelaisian gastronomic humour with tales of mercantile trickery in the manner of Ali Baba into stories of fortunes won and lost at the hands of fickle fate. Still others are suffused with motifs of magic borrowed from classical mythology and medieval romance literature reconfigured within the idioms of folklore, for the fairy-tale narrative comprises above all the changeling figure of metamorphosis. Each of Straparola's stories concludes with a riddle of elliptical double entendre, like a Renaissance parlour game, which all the company endeavours to divine. Much turns on the fortunes of family and marriage, for both men and women of every estate, often inflected by the intervention of fairy animals endowed with magical agency, of which the most celebrated is the fast-talking cat that would later become Puss-in-Boots.[2] While Straparola's fairy cat remains bootless, his stories are suffused with the details of dress and domestic appurtenance to which this section attends, in a consideration of their figurative materiality.

Throughout, Straparola's tales and jokes are bespangled with fateful objects. Lucrezia's own story is one of gifted shoes as an allegory of love – if a noble, then of velvet, if a merchant, of fine cloth, if an artisan or mechanical, of sturdy leather hide – while her riddle is that of a cobbler who must make the shoe fit his lady.[3] Whether courtly jewels, rich textiles, dress, carriages, perfumes, banqueting foods, and gardens of scented flowers, or the instruments of their making, such as golden spindles, a tailor's needle, a cobbler's last, or a pastry maker's pestle, these fairy tales figured destiny in artefactual form. The stories are densely woven with artisanal objects from the cloth of quotidian culture, howsoever magically transformed. Animals talk, an orchard apple sings, a phial of water dances, each one gifted with an enchanted animation. Details such as golden fruit and flasks of magical potion are the charmed means of restoring life when all is lost in the fairy tale's bewitched allegories of love and estate. Strange stories of metamorphic fortune, their composition is mirrored in these thaumaturgically transformative objects.

Suffused with fairy-tale transformations of poverty into wealth, Straparola's stories are quintessentially those of metamorphic reversal. Though yet without a definitive Cinderella, Straparola's fairy tales are in her image, in what scholars

---

[2] Straparola, 1550, 1553; Bottigheimer, 2002. Beecher (Straparola, 2012) and Magnanini (Straparola, 2015) offer contrasting translations.
[3] Straparola, 1550, I, V 5.

have termed sociological 'rise' tales.[4] Straparola's changeable destinies are
marked by enchanted objects of material wealth, in the case of women above
all pertaining to the bridal toilet and dress. Their narrative agency lies in each
object's enigmatic position at the threshold between the fictive and the social
realm. That is to say, the fairy-tale artefact's cultural resonance rests on its
possession of a joint imaginary, of both materiality and ethereality. It is at once
part of a social world of Renaissance goods, howsoever of the finest luxury, and
at the same time configured airily as the stuff of dreams. This quality of fantastic
materiality is manifest in overlapping and shifting ways: diamonds of impossible size; great palaces that arise overnight; or gold-silk gowns made from
cinder-rags by the touch of a magic wand. Howsoever made by an enchanted
manufacture, yet fairy-tale objects also comprise a full cultural register of the
materialist technologies of their social production, above all the instruments of
textiles and dress: the tailor's scissors, the embroiderer's needle, the spinning
wheel, the distaff, and the fabled spindle.

Though not yet tied to a definitive Sleeping Beauty narrative, many of
Straparola's stories turn on a fateful spindle, as the age-old instrument by
which to spin fibre into thread, and the narrative agent of an apparently
bewitched manufacture. Among his fairy tales, Straparola's story of Queen
Doralice unfolds around such textile objects of marital fortune. This queen is
alternately ensnared by the wiles of a merchant selling gold spindles and
distaffs, while gaining her freedom by escape in a *cassone*, the decorated bridal
chest in which Renaissance women kept their gifted matrimonial valuables of
linens and dress. Carried in wedding procession, the nuptial trousseau was the
ritualised material sign of marital estate, twining women's destinies in marriage
with its representation in cloth.[5] Many of Straparola's concluding riddles are
also of textiles and their manufacturing instruments, such as flax shuttles for
linen and needles for lace, as material allegories of female fate. Similarly, in
Straparola's account of what we may recognise as an Aladdin's tale of
a sorcerer's apprentice set within a tailor's shop, the young Dionigi learns the
arts of necromancy alongside those of cutting and sewing cloth.[6] From the
needle's eye to spinning a yarn, Straparola himself relates his stories as if woven
from the materials of destiny. Like the Arabian princess Scheherazade whose
1,001 stories lengthened the lives of herself and her female subjects by so many
nights, every inset narrative is conceived as a woven tapestry of each life.
Straparola's frontispiece illustrates an undergirding metaphor of storytelling
as spun words (**Fig. 1**). Depicting three Venetian beauties on a terrace,

---

[4] Bottigheimer, 2002; Aarne & Thompson, 1961; Propp, 1968.
[5] On Renaissance marriage, D'Elia, 2004; Bayer, 2008.
[6] Straparola, 1550, I, I 4; 1553, II, VIII 5.

Figure 1 Straparola [pseudonym], frontispiece, Clotho, Lachesis and Atropos spinning, *Piacevoli notti*, vol. 1, fol. 6, Venice, 1570 (Photo: Google Books).

Straparola's classically styled allegories of narrative are surely both the women of Lucrezia's social circle and the ancient Moirai – Clotho, Lachesis, and Atropos – those mythological embodiments of fate who spin, measure, and cut the metaphorical thread of each life in the stories they relate. As figurations of the ancient Fates, they are also *fate* – fairies – the etymological derivation of the fateful fairy agent. Straparola's tales glisten with embroidered narrative details of Renaissance textile wealth configured in fairy-tale form.

Within the frame of Straparola's stories, a range of inset narratives act as further bridges between the fictions of fairy tales and their social composition. In a reflection of the occasion of their telling at Lucrezia's behest, these tales often close with fictive entertainments to mirror her own. Many of the riddles pertain to the world of Lucrezia's hospitality, of musical instruments such as the trombone and the viola da gamba, as light metaphors of love but also their social performance among the company of guests.[7] Some stories are wrought in several languages, with a play of linguistic references in the manner of Renaissance academical gatherings, others in a range of dialects pertaining to the great literary *questione della lingua* of Renaissance authorship inaugurated by Dante. One of the riddles, purportedly related by the Venetian humanist Bernardo Cappello, is of figurative play itself in all its manifold meanings, from the comic tricks of peasant proverbs to the literary fictions of poetic myth;

---

[7] Elias, 1989.

another is the very figure of thought as 'a thing whose seeming none can tell'.[8]
Others are of the quill pen, as a corollary to the spindle's yarn and the allegorical
instrument of the author's storytelling.[9] The tale of Padre Papiro Schizza –
signifying paper, papyrus, and sketch, but also joke – is a playful battle of
intellects with a know-nothing priest who purports to great learning in a comic
medley of Latinate puns that results in cooked capons, cats' tails, and
conflagration.[10] Sixteenth-century Venice was, of course, a leading centre of
Renaissance book publishing from the mid-fifteenth-century advent of the
printing press. Its vast trade in goods from the East brought ancient Greek and
Arabic manuscripts as well as every kind of oral relay of folklore. Its burgeoning printers and booksellers forged the historic extension of literacy and literature that a 'Renaissance' periodisation as the re-birth or revival of letters has
long been understood to represent.[11] While stories of fairy-tale fate are of
diffuse and archaic origin, Straparola's collection is a Renaissance eventuality
as the first to appear in print. Republished repeatedly across the sixteenth and
seventeenth centuries, Straparola's anthology was rapidly translated into all
major European languages, inaugurated by its 1560 rendition in French.
Through Straparola, the new diffusion of the Arabian fairy tale enabled by the
printing press extended the social-intellectual pastimes of an aristocratic sociability led by women such as Lucrezia to all literate ranks.[12]

2.1 The Fairy-Tale Bride

At the conclusion to Straparola's story of Costantino Fortunato, the miller's son
who inherits nothing but the family cat by whose magical ministrations he
achieves great wealth and renown, he is wed to Princess Elisetta 'with a rich
dowry of gold and jewels and sumptuous raiment'. In a social mirror of
Renaissance marriage custom, howsoever of a fairy-tale transformation, 'when
the nuptial ceremonies were completed and the festivities at an end, the king bade
them load ten mules with gold and five with the richest garments, accompanied by
a great concourse of attendants, to her husband's house'.[13] In Straparola's
embryonic Puss-in-Boots, the comedic tale continues for, of course, Costantino
has no house, palatial or otherwise, in which to receive his bride, but for the
continuing machinations of his cat by whose means he magically acquires
a stately castle just in the nick of time. Humour and fairy-cat magic aside, the

---

[8] Straparola, 1553, II, XIII 5; IV 3.   [9] Straparola, 1553, II, VI 2.
[10] Straparola, 1553, II, IX 4.
[11] From an extensive scholarship: King, 2014; Hale, 1973; Eisenstein, 2012; Celenza, 2018; Yates,
1947, on the ludic sociability of Renaissance academicals.
[12] Dooley, 2016, on Straparola's female readers.
[13] Straparola, 1553, II, XI 1, translation adapted from Beecher (Straparola, 2012, II, 211).

account of Elisetta's bridal procession with her trousseau of textiles and gold carried by mules from her father's to her husband's home is the defining symbolic ritual of Renaissance marriage, marking the publicly displayed transfer of the bride along with her dowry. As a gift in return, the groom prepares the marital chamber in advance for her reception, whether as newly built or remodelled apartments for their life as a couple, or simply the ritualised decoration of their future abode. In fairy-tale form, *The Thousand and One Nights* is similarly suffused with descriptions of marriage and dowry exchange, of impossible matrimonial castles built of gemstones, or the sweetmeats and sherbets of a wedding feast and the glittering raiment of jewelled bridal dress. The conclusion of the *Arabian Nights* results in Scheherazade's own royal marriage, alongside that of her sister, celebrated with a succession of *divertissements* performed by the two princesses in a display of music and dance garbed in dazzling dresses of rainbow-silks and jewels.[14] Howsoever the stuff of fairy tales in their wondrous accounts of banquets served on platters of massy gold, horses caparisoned in gem-encrusted trappings, and brides dressed as queens, there are within these descriptions the readily discernible rituals and dowry goods of social custom. The culturally recognisable and most conspicuous point of their convergence, then as now, is royal marriage. The fairy-tale royal wedding may be said to invoke marriage's dream-like aspiration, founded in the ceremonial splendour of queenship.

Among the best-documented of sixteenth-century princely weddings was that of Ferdinando de' Medici to the French princess Christine of Lorraine, grand-daughter to Queen Catherine de Médicis (as well as the royal princess of Denmark) and thus heir to the princely cultures of both Florence and France. Celebrated in the Cathedral of Florence in 1589, the month-long entertainments, composed of balls, banquets, parades, tournaments, concerts, masquerades, and theatre, were a year in preparation involving all the artists and artisans of the Medici court and were attended by thousands of guests. While the bridal progress of a princess was in important respects markedly different from those of other social registers, it was nonetheless the symbolic transfer of women from maidenhood to matrimony. Accounts document the magnificent textile embellishment for the occasion: dresses of spun gold encrusted in jewels, costume decorations of sequins, rosettes, silk-embroidered flowers, bells, tinsel, fringes, lace edging, ruffs, feathers, ribbons, and buttons, set onto thousands of yards of silk-satins, velvets, taffetas, patterned damasks, fine sarcenets, and gauzy *veli*. While the dyers and tailors of this magnificent display were men, the seamstresses, embroiderers, and ribbon-, button-, and lacemakers were women,

---

[14] Galland, 1704–17, XII.

largely working in the cottage industries of either conventual or family employ-
ment. In mercantile terms, the textile preparations involved every social register, from the Florentine patricians Strozzi, Salviati, and Guicciardini to the
swathes of artisans in their employ. The extensive court encomia of their
description concern not only a wondrous apprehension of the fabulous luxury
of their materials, but also the seemingly magical means of their making.[15] Just
as the figure of the royal bride was one of occasion, the goods that marked her
now-marital status were intended as lifelong and even dynastic heirloom possessions. Through the imaginary objects of fairy-tale brides, we may enter the
social field of their royal production, without any need to rupture literature's
fictions. As the province of queens and their appointed artisans in the making of
'fairy-tale' luxuries, the objects' exquisite facture, howsoever veiled in
a language of the marvellous, is at the same time one of social composition:
of weavers, spinners, dyers, seamstresses, tailors, embroiderers, lacemakers,
hosiers, featherers, ribbon-makers, glove-makers, wig-makers, jewellers, gold-
and silversmiths, furriers, cobblers, tanners, glass- and mirror-makers, wheel-
wrights, carriage- and livery-makers, those artisanal trades and retainers of
Renaissance princely manufacturing.[16]

Fairy-tale accounts of metamorphic fortune in which cinder-girls became
queens are also, however lightly, haunted by their social opposite. Cinderella's
fall at the hands of her stepmother speaks to the great variegations of women's
fortunes within Renaissance cultural practices of arranged marriages and child
brides, at all social levels, as well as the destitutions of abuse and poverty for
abandoned women in the cyclical famines of a pre-modern era.[17] In a fairy-tale
configuration, while some women were magically transformed by marriage into
queens, fickle fate cast others into a wilderness of abjection. In Straparola's
lightly comic tale of Thia, a beautiful peasant woman who caught the eye of
a wealthy man at a country dance, he seeks her out to find her spinning flax on
a distaff. In reply to his amorous entreaty, Thia marks their differences of estate
in terms of textile and gastronomic wealth:

> You are rich, and I am poor; you are a signor, and I am a working woman; you
> can have fine ladies to your taste, and I am of low condition. You are wont to
> walk gaily with your embroidered surcoat, and your brightly-coloured hose,
> all worked with wool and silk, and I, as you see, have nothing but a dimity
> petticoat, old, torn, and mended . . . . You eat wheaten loaves, and I rye-bread

---

[15] Saslow, 1996, 73–84; Warburg, 1999.
[16] From an extensive scholarship: Gerritsen & Riello, 2015; Smith, 2004; Vries, 2003, 2010; Jones &
Stallybrass, 2000; Welch, 2017; Griffey, 2019; Arizzoli-Clémentel & Gorguet Ballesteros, 2009;
Roche, 1994; Schneider, 1989.
[17] Ó Gráda, with Alfani, 2017.

and beans and polenta, and even then often not enough . . .. We toil hard to till
the earth and to sow our wheat, which you fine folk consume.[18]

In Straparola's humorous account it is Thia who mocks the menfolk, both
rich and poor, tricking the wealthy man into gifts of fat capons and by means of
mock magic hiding her husband's head in a corn measure. The concluding
riddle of a cattle yoke is surely with reference to the straits and wiles of
marriage as well as those of Thia's agricultural labour. In the story of Thia,
howsoever in comic vein, textile wealth is a matter of estate, as also is its
production. This is further marked in terms of gender as a domestic industry of
women's work. Thia spins flax and tends to the vines in her garden. Her labour
provides the table and dress of the rich, while she herself is subject to the
vagaries of fortune's harvest. Her tale is one of minor reversal in a life of
perpetual want.

Within Straparola's literary rendition of such folkloric stories, if the particular industries of textiles were divided by estate and gender, as to fulling and
dying, weaving and spinning, yet they were just as often knit together in
symbolic terms. Fine needlework embroidery was the social province of noble-
women and queens as well as artisans, in which both royal and peasant women
embroidered and stitched their cloth in allegorical narratives of their lives and
livelihoods. Similarly, Straparola's female narrators, as archetypal Venetian
beauties, configured their social identity as storytellers in terms of both the
pen and the needle, for they wove and span their yarns with the thread of their
words. Among literary genres, the fairy tale is thus a complex cultural prism of
social relations, particularly between men and women in the constitution of
marriage and family, and related questions of economic wealth production and
distribution. Within the emblematic fairy-tale object, social relations also take
on their fantastic form of magical reversal.

In addressing the broader artisanal and mercantile histories of Renaissance
manufacturing, this account of the fairy-tale object is not, then, innocent of the
social circumstances of its making, nor of its considered twentieth-century
critiques.[19] On the contrary, this analysis seeks to uncover the literary and
material production of a Renaissance trade in luxury goods within the conjoined
prisms of cultural and economic history, as the products of exchange as well as

---

[18] Straparola, 1550, I, V 4, translation by Beecher (Straparola, 2012, I, 261–2).

[19] Modern critique of the fairy-tale genre encompasses a wide-ranging interdisciplinary spectrum:
Bettelheim, 1975; Propp, 1968; Darnton, 2009; the important feminist critique launched by
Lieberman, 1972; Tatar, 1992; Warner, 1994; Seifert, 2004. Swann Jones, 1995, 119–40; Zipes,
2001; Tatar, 1995; Greenhill and colleagues, 2018; Teverson, 2019 offer analytical overviews.
Specifically dedicated to Cinderella narratives, Dundes, 1983; Hennard Dutheil de la Rochère,
2016; Rozario, 2018. On fairy-tale artefacts, Hoffmann, 2016; Reddan, 2016; Bloom, 2022.

manufacturing. It was the quest for luxury's raw materials – above all silk and gold – which drove the competitive commercial globalisation of the Renaissance European crowns. Sponsoring voyages of exploration as a means of extending their empires of exchange, the economics of Renaissance trading were those of colonialist resource-stripping, in which precious raw materials were sought through barter, enforced prestation, and slave labour for European manufacture at vast profit at home. In matters of gender and social estate as of economic colonialisms, the fairy-tale object and its ceremonial counterpart were therefore predicated on a concerted global mercantilism in the Renaissance sequestration of raw materials for the production of luxuries.[20] Like the story of Straparola's Thia, their manufacture also rested on the labour of thousands of unknown men and women. It was their collective industry, from the cinder-girl who fed the fires of Renaissance manufacturing to the courtly needlework of queens, the *coureur des bois* seeking furs in the Canadian wilderness, the African ivory elephant-hunter, and the slaves who mined Potosí silver, which forged the fairy-tale character of Renaissance *luxe*.

2.2 The Toilet of Venus

Among Straparola's 'cinderella' fairy tales is that of a baker's daughter, Chiaretta, who marries a king only to be cast out to the scullery.[21] To redeem their mother, her sons must secure three magical objects. The first is a fountain of dancing water, captured in a glass phial. Next, they must fetch a singing apple guarded by a serpent. Attiring themselves in robes of mirrors, they bedazzle and transfix the monster in its own reflection. At last, they must find a talking parakeet, though they are first transformed into marble statues from which only the bird's brightest feather can release them. In the marbling powers of its mirror-imagery, the story plays lightly on the classical myth of Medusa and Perseus, as of the golden apples in the Garden of Hesperides, while the concluding riddle of an emerald bird in a gilded cage causes the company to invoke the romance of Orlando in a guessing-game of love's trials and the gentle confines of marriage. In Cristoforo Armeno's fairy-tale account of the *Three Princes of Serendip*, similarly of Persian origin and published in Venice only a few years after Straparola, serendipitous fate leads them on a quest for knowledge through which they acquire their destinies. In their travels to India, they divine the fortunes of a camel, give ingenious answers to a courtly riddle concerning a bewitched crystal mountain of rock-salt, and rescue the

---

[20] On early modern *luxe*: Vries, 2003, 2008, 2010; Roche, 1994. On decolonising the fairy tale, Haase, 2010; Lau, 2016.

[21] Straparola, 1550, I, IV 3.

kingdom from a terrible curse by means of a magic mirror.[22] Straparola's tale of Prince Livoretto and his fairy-horse is also one of royal fortune through enchanted artefacts in which he must court Princess Belissandra by finding her gold ring, and bringing her a glass flask filled from an enchanted fountain of life-giving waters.[23] Pygmalion-like, Princess Belissandra then makes a pie in his image, sprinkling it with the bewitched water to revive it in a metamorphic allegory of his life remade in her. In the story of Doralice, the prince-in-waiting Fortunio wins the princess through a series of jousting competitions in which he appears in armour studded with jewels, and he and his horse caparisoned in gold-embroidered satin. When he is abducted by the sea, Doralice restores him with the gift of precious crafted apples in bronze, silver, and gold, so that he may be transformed into an eagle and return to her.[24]

As Straparola's text redolently illustrates, Venice and its islands were a site of exalted patrician architecture, of lavish interiors and lush gardens fitted for all manner of elite entertainment, to which its extensive scholarship in architectural history and domestic furnishing amply testifies. As a consequence Venice was also a much-vaunted centre for luxury manufactured goods, ornaments, and artefacts of every kind, from fine wines and *pasticcerie* to jewellery, lace, and silks for dress and furnishings.[25] In respect of its seafaring position, it was Italy's leading centre of Eastern trade in imported coffee, salt, sugar, and spices, as well as for Oriental pearls and gemstones, Persian carpets, and decorative woods, inaugurated with the mercantile traveller's tales of Marco Polo.[26] Travel and trade brought not only material goods, but also cultural exchange, as manifest in the transmission of Arabian fairy tales. In its manufacturing, Venice was also host to the production of the most valuable Renaissance textiles, from patterned silk-velvets, damasks, and brocades, to cloth of gold and silver woven with precious metals, while the finest Venetian lace was made from flaxen thread on the little island of Burano. Alongside costly mineral pigments, imported from the East, came glowing ground-gemstone enamelwork and mosaic from the Levant. Renaissance Venice was also Europe's leading centre for luxury glassware, in imitation of Middle Eastern manufactures, which emanated from the blown-glass workshops of Straparola's Murano.

Like the Cinderella story of fateful transformation, Renaissance glass as a material spanned a full social spectrum, from workaday kitchen jars to the finest luxury tableware of queens. Known from antiquity, then falling into some desuetude, glassmaking was revived in the late Middle Ages and thereafter dispersed across Europe to become a leading Renaissance manufacture.

---

[22] Armeno, 1557. [23] Straparola, 1550, I, III 2. [24] Straparola, 1550, I, III 4.
[25] From an extensive scholarship: Fortini Brown, 2004; Molà, 2000; Allerston, 1998.
[26] Lanaro, 2006.

Figure 2 Venetian c. 1500, blown-glass gourd or pilgrim flask with enamelling, Metropolitan Museum of Art (Photo: Metropolitan Museum of Art).

As Syria was always the source of the finest glass, Venetian glassmaking prospered from its Levantine trade with renewed strength from the thirteenth century on, following the Sack of Constantinople in 1204, of Damascus in 1400, and its fall to the Ottomans in 1453.[27] The dominance of Middle Eastern glass across the Middle Ages is reflected in the cultural diffusion of its decorative enamelwork patterns and colours to the Venetian Renaissance manufactures (**Fig. 2**). The accelerating growth of Venetian glassmaking within the late medieval urban fabric led the city rulers to reposition its production to the outlying island of Murano in 1291, closely followed by lacemaking to neighbouring Burano.

A Renaissance expansion of European luxury glass manufacture was, in the first instance, tied to the development of princely tableware that accompanied

---

[27] Carboni & Whitehouse, 2001.

an ever-augmented courtly etiquette, so ushering in the historical elaboration of the dinner service with its attendant glassware, often as betrothal or wedding gifts.[28] Glass beads of every colour, including gold and silver, were made in imitation of precious metals and gemstones, as jewellery and in the gem-like ornamentation of the most expensive textiles. Known as *conterie*, glass- and mirror-beads were also increasingly used as a form of mercantile currency in the Serenissima's global trading, especially in the Americas and Africa.[29] Glass also made its way into the domestic decorative arts, in particular, of gifted luxury toiletries for the sumptuous dressing tables of merchant-princes, nobles, and royalty. Witness to its princely patronage, Murano's illustrious clients comprised Isabella d'Este, Ferdinand and Isabella of Spain, and the Medicean French Queen Catherine, among a constellation of European royalty.[30] According to the Venetian chronicler Marin Sanudo, Murano's starred glassworks became a celebrated attraction for courtly visitors of all kinds, including the Queen of France, Anne of Brittany, in 1502, Charles Bourbon, Duke of Vendôme, in 1515, Federico Gonzaga, the future Duke of Mantua, in 1517, Cardinal Ippolito d'Este, in 1520, Alfonso d'Este, Duke of Ferrara, in 1531, and Francesco Maria della Rovere, Duke of Urbino, in 1532.[31]

Forged in fire from vitreous sand mixed with ash, the molten-liquid glass as it emerged from the furnace could be blown into glistening globules of ever greater size and complex form with the gathering artisanal expertise of Murano's glass-makers.[32] Its changeable materiality, from solid to liquid and back, was readily absorbed within Renaissance cultures of metamorphic-alchemical enquiry, as also its shimmering evanescence, in a paradigm of purportedly magical artisanal chemistry. Its oscillating materiality was conceived within fairy-tale allegories of changing fortune, like the miller's blonde daughter consigned to spin straw into gold with the aid of a puckish goblin that would later become Rumpelstiltskin. Murano glass was particularly valued for an almost immaterial ethereality, resulting from ever finer attenuation in its blown facture, and for its crystalline transparence with the introduction of herbal and mineral bleaching ingredients in the paste. It was named *cristallo* glass in recognition of its much-vaunted imitation of the gems it was valued by. Glass could also be infused with all the precious mineral pigments to produce a sparkling material of endlessly variable colouring, further enhanced by decoration in lustrous enamelwork and gilding in silver and gold.

---

[28] Strong, 2002.   [29] Zecchin, 1987–90, III, especially 368–71; Trivellato, 2000.
[30] Zecchin, 1987–90, II, 273–8; Trivellato, 2000.   [31] Zecchin, 1987–90, II, 273–8.
[32] Zecchin, 1987–90; Hess & Wight, 2005.

In Straparola's fairy-tale transformations of cinder-girls into queens, the ritual objects of the nuptial toilet play a fateful part in the preparation of the bride's venereal beauty. In this, he echoes the jewelled nuptial toilets of the Arabian fairy tales, as in the story of Aladdin, dressing princesses before looking glasses in necklaces of pearls, bracelets of rubies, and girdles beset with diamonds by their ladies' maids, who also shower them in flowered perfumes. These stories are suffused with the scent of violet, jasmine, eglantine, narcissus, myrtle, and willow-flower, mixed with ambergris and musk. Venetian trade to the East made it a leading centre of Renaissance cosmetics and particularly scented infusions of exotic spices and flora. These were costly, for each pound of scented oil or water required thousands of blossoms, of which rose, lavender, and lily were among the most sought after.[33] Scents were kept in bijoux glass bottles ornamented with ivory, enamelling, precious metals, and gemstones, configured for the dressing tables of brides as of queens (**Figs. 3** and **4**).[34] Perfumed oils and waters were also sprinkled on clothes, rugs, linens, and furnishings, for purposes of good health as well as olfactory pleasure. Cosmetic oils and waters were further conceived within a medicinal use of herbals in the treatment of hair and skin for both health and beauty, and so closely linked to the apothecary's *pharmacopoeia*. The Venetian physician Giovanni Marinelli's *Ornaments for Beautiful Women* of 1562 was one of many manuals of herbal recipes on the dressing of hair and the preparation of the female toilet of perfumed bathing, and colouring of the eyes, lips, face, and skin, as a treatise of ideal beauty in practice.[35] Similarly, a 1555 book of perfume recipes by Giovanni Ventura Rosetti arose from his work at the Arsenale shipyards with oversight of their incoming goods. He also published a book on herbal and mineral colour-dyes for cosmetics as for textiles, paints, enamel, and stained or coloured glass.[36] Such luxury toiletries were much-represented in sixteenth-century Venetian painting, in a rich flowering of *belle donne* portraits lightly allegorised as depictions of the goddess Venus at her toilet. Often commissioned as patrician marital gifts for the decoration of the nuptial chamber, the genre first became manifest in Venice circa 1500 with celebrated examples by Giovanni Bellini, the young Titian, Veronese, and Tintoretto, and subsequently a wide dispersion across the courts of Europe (**Fig. 5**).[37] Ivory combs and bodkins set with enamels and jewels, glass scent-bottles and ewers cased in silver and gold caging, decorated mirrors, pearls, and fine linens were fitting ornament to the female toilet. Equally, the lavish toiletry objects they depicted were themselves in imitation of luxury

---

[33] Bimbenet-Privat, 2009; Le Guérer, 2005.   [34] Carré & Lagabrielle, 2019.
[35] Marinelli, 1562; Nocentini, 2010.   [36] Rosetti, 1548; Rosetti, 1555.
[37] Aikema, 2009; Bayer, 2008; Ferino-Pagden, 2006.

Figure 3 Crystal scent-bottle with reverse-glass painting and gilding, sixteenth-century Lombard, Susannah and the Elders, Kunsthistorisches Museum Vienna (Photo: Kunsthistorisches Museum Vienna).

Renaissance wedding gifts, often from the groom to his bride, and emblems of the venereal transformation of women that marriage brought.

Within Straparola's Murano stories, such luxury toiletries are emblematically described among the artefactual metaphors of nuptial beauty. At the close of Princess Belissandra's marriage with Prince Livoretto, the concluding riddle is of a dainty glass phial of rose water, in a courtly (if entirely derivative) poetic emulation of the healing flask of enchanted water of life he won for her:

Figure 4 Fortuna flask, Venetian sixteenth-century blue glass perfume gourd
with Limoges enamelling and gilding, Musée du Louvre
(Photo: Réunion des Musées Nationaux).

> Small though my compass be
> A mighty furnace gendered me
> It is a liquor soft and sweet
> All silken are my festal clothes.[38]

The ensuing guessing-game turns on a gentle comedy of the bridal toilet, allegorised in a glass vase of floral scent. This is echoed in a number of Straparola's tales containing flasks of charmed herbal cosmetic water, in which the boundary between the social and the fictional realm is a particularly resonant one, for the quest for magically infused elixirs of longevity and beauty

---

[38] Straparola, 1550, I, III 2, translation by Beecher (Straparola, 2012, I, 399).

Figure 5 Jacopo Robusti Tintoretto, *Susannah and the Elders*, oil on canvas, Kunsthistorisches Museum Vienna (Photo: Wikimedia).

was a lively concern of the Renaissance *pharmacopoeia*. The cultural conception of perfume as a tonic for both hygiene and beauty flourished particularly with the sixteenth-century development of distilled alcohol – *acqua vita* or eau de vie – as a foundation for scent in lieu of oil, notably in the celebrated *eau de la reine* made for the 1533 nuptials of Catherine de' Medici to Henri II of France. In Paris, the physician André Le Fournier's 1530 treatise on female beauty advocated apparently transformative dermatological recipes such as bathing in milk distilled with cinnamon and egg to lend a glow of good health. Other recipes advised milk-white baths for hygiene and skin healing composed of vinegar and lead oxide, also used to lighten skin and hair, along with lemon.[39] Straparola's Biancabella echoes this in the story of a princess who is maimed and blinded by cruel fate only to be restored by means of magical bathing in fine vases of milk and then rose water as the prelude to her nuptials.[40] In the august painted representation of the Venetian Renaissance female toilet as the Toilet of Venus, from Titian to all the courts of Europe and particularly France, precious silvered-crystal and glass phials of scent or cosmetics are often accompanied by decorative glass mirrors, as the material signs of an enchanted beauty.

---

[39] Fournier, 1530.   [40] Straparola, 1550, I, III 3.

Straparola's stories of nuptial rituals capture a much-celebrated Venetian Renaissance *bellezza* in fairy-tale form.

Like the ornamental perfume jar, the decorated glass mirror was also a fairy-tale object of the bridal toilet. In the *Arabian Nights'* story of prince Zeyn Alasnam of Balsora, a magical mirror of marital destiny gifted by the King of the Genii is the means of finding his bride, whose diamond-like beauty lights the vault of his treasury like his life.[41] In other stories, the looking glass is the locus of scented and bejewelled nuptial toilets as the usher to love. Within social custom, precious perfume bottles and silvered pocket-mirrors alike were aristocratic spousal gifts, framed and worn as jewelled compacts attached by silk ribbon to the feminine girdle of the waist as the material signs of intimacy and betrothal (**Figs. 6** and **7**).[42] Concomitantly, princely inventories of crown jewels across the Renaissance also detail gifted Murano scent-bottles and mirrors set with pearl and precious stones in both ebony and gold. Henri IV's minister, Maximilien de Béthune, the Duke of Sully, recounted in his *Mémoires* a gift to Elizabeth I of a Venetian mirror encased in a gold cover encrusted with diamonds as a princely prestation. François I had also commissioned mirrors of silver-foiled rock crystal or Venetian *cristallo* glass from his royal jewellers, further decorated with precious stones and framed in ebony or gold as gifts.[43] Feminine toiletry objects were celebrated by court poets from Petrarch and Bembo to Shakespeare and the French Pléiade in the circle of Pierre de Ronsard, in which the authors longed to rival their lady's instruments of beauty – her ivory comb, her mirror, her scent, her 'happy jewels' – for intimate admission to her person.[44]

The Renaissance art of the toilet was particularly prized at Fontainebleau, in imitation of both ancient and Venetian *bellezze*. François I's bucolic Fontainebleau palace was suffused with the luxuries of courtly bathing as a social occasion in emulation of the ancients. Its celebrated baths were lavishly decorated with painted mythological scenes of Venus bathing, marked also in lightly allegorised court imagery of *la belle au bain*, pictured amid a sumptuous display of jewels, textiles, and richly decorated toiletries of gilded ornament comprising ewers, mirrors, and bottled perfume (**Fig. 8**).[45] Similarly, in the heraldic tapestries of aristocratic marriage known as *The Lady and the Unicorn*, the culminating scene, *A MON SEUL DESIR*, depicts a lady-in-waiting

---

[41] Galland, 1709, 8, 33.   [42] Forsyth, 2013.

[43] Havard, 1887, 'glace', 'miroir', II, 1100–15 & III, 887–912; Thépaut-Cabasset & Warner, 2007–8.

[44] Goodman-Soeller, 1983.

[45] Fagnart, 2016. Paintings on display are thought to have included Leonardo's *Mona Lisa*, *La belle ferronière*, and the lost *Leda*.

Figure 6 Scent-bottle, sixteenth-century Cheapside Hoard, milk opal with gold and gemstone decoration, Museum of London (Photo: Museum of London).

proffering a casket of jewels for her lady's toilet beneath a tented canopy decorated in royal *fleur-de-lys,* while an earlier scene represents her holding a richly worked gold hand mirror framed by gemstones (**Fig. 9**).[46] Like the spindle that surely wove the silken threads of the tapestry's making, these are textile representations of her betrothal gifts through which to narrate the lady's marital progress. The fairy-tale objects of an enchanted material luxury were of a social composition, woven from the cloth of culture into lustrous coloured silk.

---

[46] Pastoureau & Taburet-Delahaye, 2013.

Figure 7 Jewelled dress mirror, sixteenth-century French jewellery-work, glass and gold with enamel, pearls, garnets, and sapphires, Musée de la Renaissance, Château d'Ecouen (Photo: Réunion des Musées Nationaux).

2.3 The Cinderella Affair

In Honoré de Balzac's great compendia of literary genres, *La comédie humaine* (1829–48), the nineteenth-century French novelist brought together an array of stories and essays in imitation of Boccaccio, as a panoramic 'portrait of society' concerned with national destiny alongside the rise and fall of individual fortunes. Among them was an enquiry into the life of the sixteenth-century Florentine queen of France, Catherine de Médicis (**Fig. 10**).Written in the form of an historical *novella*, it prompted Balzac to pronounce on what would

Figure 8 School of Fontainebleau, *Toilet of Venus,* oil on canvas, Musée du Louvre (Photo: Wikimedia).

Figure 9 *The Lady and the Unicorn,* Flemish c. 1500, wool and silk-thread tapestry, Musée de Cluny (Photo: Alamy).

Figure 10 Portrait of Henri II and Catherine de Médicis, sixteenth-century French School, Musée du Chateau d'Anet (Photo: Getty Images).

become a heated late nineteenth-century French cultural debate dubbed the 'Cinderella Affair'. Balzac's point of reference was the version of the Cinderella fairy tale published in Paris in 1697 under the pseudonym of the proverbial nursemaid, Mother Goose, but in fact long acknowledged as the work of Perrault, French courtier and literary academician to Louis XIV, and capable secretary to the king's first minister, Jean-Baptiste Colbert. Titled *Cinderella, or the Little Glass Slipper*, Perrault's version introduced the fairy-tale glass shoe as the defining motif of the cinder-girl's magical transformation into a royal bride, just as he would also give Straparola's fairy cat of good fortune his distinctive pair of boots.[47]

---

[47] Perrault, 1981, 171–8. On their early publication history and textual variations, see Perrault, 1999, edited by Froloff; while Jones' edition stresses questions of gender. On Perrault, Bouchenot-Déchin, 2018; and his *Mémoires de ma vie*, Perrault, 1759; on Perrault and the early modern French fairy tale, Robert, 1982; and subsequent scholarly editions of his corpus.

Balzac's interest in Perrault's Cinderella arose within his study of the Renaissance fur trade, as an aspect of Queen Catherine's royal luxury contingent on a globalising European quest for precious materials that drove the early history of circumnavigation and marked the sixteenth century as an age of exploration:

> certain rare furs, such as *vair*, which was beyond doubt imperial sable, might be worn only by kings, dukes, and men of high rank holding certain offices. *Vair* (a name still used in heraldry ...) was subdivided into *grand vair* and *menu vair*. The word has [fallen] so completely into disuse, that in hundreds of editions of Perrault's fairy-tales, Cinderella's famous slipper, probably of fur, *menu vair*, has become a glass slipper, *pantoufle de verre*.[48]

Seemingly unaware or unconvinced of Perrault's original typography, Balzac sought to materialise in historical terms the evanescent glass slipper of Perrault's fairy-tale account into one made of fur. Within the nineteenth century's burgeoning interest in fairy tales, Balzac's claim proved incendiary. The 'Cinderella Affair' was waged in Parisian print with any number of literary commentators, among them Anatole France's light-hearted defence of a glass slipper as the very stuff of *contes de fées*.[49] While France was surely correct to insist on the impossible materialities of fairy tales (lightly punning on Cinderella's slippers as *fée/fait*) yet Balzac's query of *verre* as *vair*, if incorrectly and arguably inadvertently, touched on the Erasmian complexity of Perrault's fabled lexicon. In the rich double entendre of his language, Perrault's magisterial '*pantoufle de verre*' brought together into a concerted oscillation of meaning not only thick fur with transparent glass, but also a social history of Renaissance trade in luxury artefacts and materialities with its figurative counterpart of enchanted objects. For, if Perrault's Cinderella story is one of magical manufactures, it mirrored the social world of Renaissance artisanship. Most directly, it encapsulated in miniature Colbert's mercantilist economic policy in the establishment of the French luxury manufactures – above all, the fabled glass of Louis' Hall of Mirrors at Versailles (**Fig. 11**).[50] Thus Perrault's detail of Cinderella's glass slipper is a figured microcosm of the conceptual, material, and cultural materialities that structured Louis XIV's national economy in the palatial fabrication of French *luxe*.

2.4 Manufactures

Within the fairy-tale fiction of a glass slipper, and also Balzac's historical enquiry into its making (however paradoxical), lies a material history of

---

[48] Balzac, 1901, 49. Hoffmann, 2016, 66–72.   [49] France, 1955, 165.
[50] Milovanovic & Volle, 2013; Milovanovic & Maral, 2007.

Figure 11 Jules Hardouin-Mansart, *Hall of Mirrors*, 1678–84, Château de Versailles (Photo: Wikimedia).

Renaissance manufacturing that Perrault, as secretary to Colbert, with particular oversight for outfitting the royal palaces, would have witnessed at first hand. For, couched within the magical motif of Perrault's fairy-tale slipper was precisely the dominion of French luxury goods that Louis XIV sought to promote, especially of textiles and glass, the very materials of Cinderella's fabled dress. As Louis XIV's first minister of finance, Colbert's considered restructuring of the French economy over the 1660s and 1670s was one of mercantilist ambition, in line with larger pan-European economic thought and practice on the concerted orchestration of a French luxury economy. Colbert's commercial policies would favour the lucrative export of French manufactured goods as a highly successful means of bolstering the national coffers. Mercantilism advocated strong national reserves of currency accrued through competitive international trade, nowhere more so than in the realm of luxury industries which Colbert rightly regarded as the keystone to French economic ascendance. The exorbitant expense of importing foreign luxuries thus drove a nascent French nationalisation of the artisanal manufactures as part of Colbert's broader economic policy. At Colbert's accession in 1661, Italian luxury goods led the market, particularly textiles and Venetian glass, while, by the end of Louis' reign, in 1715, it was instead France that dominated the production of fashionable *luxe*. Due to their great expense, glass mirrors were among the earliest of Colbert's targeted restructurings of the French luxury economy, first, with the establishment of a French manufactory in 1665 and, then, by outlawing any foreign imports in 1672. The measure of his success was complete. At Louis' accession, Venetian glass had held effective monopoly of the European market for luxury glassware, and notably mirrors, for some 150 years, at vast prices reckoned at 30,000 *livres* a year for the French court. At Louis' death in 1715, France instead led Europe in glass-mirror production, exporting them at a value of some 300,000–400,000 *livres* per annum.[51] This was emblematised in Louis' Hall of Mirrors of Versailles as French mirrors-of-state, as also in the metaphorical glass slipper of Perrault's Cinderella.

The question of Renaissance luxury consumption, as much scholarship on the subject attests, had long preoccupied rulers and policy makers, for it was generally perceived as an excessive drain on finances, both individual and national. While all governments sought to promote production and export, they also strove to contain domestic consumption. Much Renaissance legislation concerning luxury goods, particularly of dress, as Balzac recognised, took the form of sumptuary laws.[52] These were chiefly concerned with constraint to highly restricted social circles of court in order to maintain clear distinctions of rank, as well as to bolster bullion reserves. Straparola narrates the preoccupations of sumptuary legislation in comic form, in a story of a young bride's over-eager acquisition of dress and her husband's playful, if vain, attempts to impose limits on her spending.[53] Although sumptuary law was chiefly a Renaissance economy, it would also continue into Colbert's policy-making, in his consideration of luxury as exclusive to royal magnificence in the representation of monarchy. In other respects, however, while sumptuary prohibition continued to be legislated, Colbert shifted his focus to economic support for native French industries in the form of tax incentives and prohibitions. This is epitomised in his orchestration of textiles, particularly for tapestries and upholstery, at the manufactory of the Gobelins, and glass mirrors at what would become St Gobain. In his supervision of the king's palaces, where Perrault would serve Colbert most directly, the Gobelins produced French textiles for interior decoration to replace import from Flanders, while the crown glassworks cast windows and mirrors to undercut Venice in the name of France.

Colbert's fiscal and commercial reforms would fully embody the concept of 'political economy' first coined by Antoine de Montchrétien's eponymous treatise of 1615, to forge a system of national wealth production for France.[54] Colbert reduced internal tariffs in favour of nationalising ones and promoted French industries both at home and abroad. Industrial technology in

---

[51] Scoville, 2008; Cole, 1939.　　[52] Riello & Rublack, 2019.　　[53] Straparola, 1550, I II 4.
[54] Montchrétien, 1615.

manufacturing was a scientific achievement Colbert sought to advance, through a planned series of publications with engraved illustrations under the auspices of the newly formed Academy of Sciences, to demonstrate French national supremacy. Albeit, only achieved some 100 years later, in Denis Diderot and Jean le Rond d'Alembert's *Encyclopaedia of the Arts*, Colbert's visionary intention was precisely the promotion of French prowess in artisanal manufacturing as the economic product of its leading research in science and technology.[55] In Perrault's position as secretary to Colbert, and specifically in the furnishing of the royal residences, he was at the fulcrum of these fiscal and administrative reforms to luxury commerce and industry. His fairy-tale account of Cinderella's fabled dress and shoes arose at the centre of Colbert's orchestration of French *luxe*.

2.5 The *querelle des femmes*

As a courtly paradigm of royal progress into queenship, Perrault's *Cinderella* touched on the myriad social roles of women, within and beyond the French court he served. Here, Perrault's *Apologie des femmes* of 1694 forms a critical context. Written in defence of the role of women within French literary cultures, it specifically concerned the chiefly female-authored literature of the Parisian *salon* and the cultural prominence of women within its female-led conversational sociability. Perrault's *Apology* was, in the first instance, written in response to his fellow academician Nicolas Boileau-Despréaux's excoriating attack on female literary production, including its fairy tales, in a debate that would become known as the *querelle des femmes*. For Perrault's reworking of the Cinderella story arose precisely within those *salon* cultures in which aristocratic women alongside men launched literary careers, and in which the favoured forms were those of *divertissements*, designed as light commentary on courtly mores. This would culminate above all in the revered figure of Madeleine de Scudéry as the first woman and renowned *salonnière* to receive the French Academy's literary prize, for her myriad textual *Conversations*, *Illustrious Women*, and specifically for her *Discourse on Glory*. Among her many cultural legacies was that of her *salon protégée* and heir, daughter to Louis' royal historiographer, Perrault's niece and fellow fairy-tale author, Mademoiselle Marie-Jeanne L'Héritier de Villandon. In the image of Princess Scheherazade, L'Héritier de Villandon conceived of her *salon* fairy tales as a form of 'enchanted eloquence'.[56] Apparently literary bagatelles, yet they carried wittily conceived allegories of fortune in court

---

[55] Diderot & D'Alembert, 2002; Knothe, 2009; Sewell, 1986.
[56] L'Héritier de Villandon, 1696.

politics as in marriage and inheritance, as Straparola's Lucrezia had also known. The questions raised by the literary *querelle des femmes* are therefore central to any discussion of early modern female authorship.[57] In Perrault, the question of female authorship pertained to his wider academic discourse on the relationship between history and futurity elaborated in his *Parallel of Ancients and Moderns*. A considered comparison between the cultural achievements of antiquity and those of the *grand siècle*, it was key to the complexity of debate in the age of Louis. A multi-volume paeon to Louis' modernity, published during 1688–92, it concerned both affinities and developments between the classical past and the present in forging a modern French culture.[58] Perrault thus tied the progressive view of women's literature to a nascent French modernism.

In Perrault's *Cabinet of the Arts* of 1690, he also wrote in defence of the artisanal or 'mechanical' crafts as liberal arts like his own. In homage to Louis XIV, Colbert, and the Academy that sponsored him, Perrault understood the arts and letters alongside the applied manufactures as fully equivalent. In his decorously nuanced commentary on the nature of the arts, Perrault brought together allegories of Eloquence in the person of the Academy, with Poetry, Music, Architecture, Painting, Sculpture; but also the applied sciences of Mechanics and Optics. His larger point, founded in his longstanding service to the Crown as academician, man of letters, as well as eminent secretary to much of Colbert's enterprise with the manufactories, was to argue the cause not only of the moderns, but of science, technology, and commerce, and thereby the position of the manufacturing arts as the equal of his own. Above all, Perrault sought to insist on the status of the luxury artisanship of Colbert's manufactures, alongside the powerful immateriality of literary words at the French Academy.[59]

As a material history, howsoever fictional, Perrault's Cinderella narrates the place of luxury objects in fairy-tale allegories of commerce and fortune in the age of Louis. Changeable fate transforms her from favoured to displaced daughter and then into a princess robed in glittering ball gowns with glass slippers. On the one hand, it is a story of starry metamorphosis, clothing her in exquisite confections of a fairy-tale facture; at the same time, it is haunted by the spectre of its opposite, as severe crop failure across France in the winter of 1692–3 had shown.[60] Perrault's *Cinderella* is a literary emblem of itself as fated, composed at a conceptual counterpoint between materialities and their fictions,

---

[57] Perrault, 1694a. Hannon, 1998; Duggan, 2019 & 2005; Beasley, 2006.
[58] Perrault, 1688–92.   [59] Perrault, 1690, 11; Martin, 2015.
[60] The death rate is estimated to have been circa 10 per cent of the population.

in which an impossible artefact – a glass slipper – lightly allegorised the manufactured objects of Colbert's economy of *luxe*.

Louis XIV's reign, as an ethnographic history of the period recognises, is one marked by increasingly complex cultural entanglements between people, words, and things, in which the semiotic lives of objects within an expanding trade in luxury commodities took on ever finer forms of social distinction. Situated at the apex of Louis XIV's establishment of the French manufactories, in which we recognise a vast historical intensification of early modern *luxe* commoditisation, Cinderella's story of ineffable materials and object-fictions is yet also undergirded by the folklore of their dearth in the eponymous figure of the cinder-girl. The fairy-tale object of the *salon* is thus of a particular social residue. In Perrault's account, the ethereal glass slipper is the fabulous object around which the Cinderella narrative turns. Through the finest allusions of language, as a verbal object it rests precisely at the cultural counterpoint between the tangible and intangible, the figurative and the factured, the ineffable presence of literary things.[61] Howsoever an impossible materiality, as an object-fiction it is the social hieroglyph of Cinderella's fairy-tale fate in the age of Louis. Thus, Perrault's fairy tale was at once myth and cultural commentary, folklore-cum-satire, ancient and modern, and a fictional reflection of changing socio-economic realities in the political modernisation of an *ancien régime*.

2.6 Mother Goose Tales

While Perrault's *Cinderella* immediately became the canonical version of the story, rapidly published in many editions, compilations, and translations, it also belonged to a much longer oral tradition comprising aspects of similar narratives (such as Straparola's) that would subsequently be distinguished from one another. The glass-slipper motif surely also drew on Germanic folklore's fairy-tale accounts of princesses enclosed within glass mountains, or princes consigned to fell forests with glass tools in order to save themselves and their brides, as allegories of love's trials. While there is no direct evidence Perrault was acquainted with these tales, his broad literary horizons make it likely. The Brothers Grimm's nineteenth-century account of the little cinder-girl would recount the story with a golden slipper, demonstrating that the history of these tales remained – and remains – a living one.[62] As a literary genre born of folklore, extending at least as far back as the Egyptian Pharaoh who married the slave-girl Rhodope at the sight of her slipper, the fairy-tale shoe as the agent of

---

[61] Fowles, 2010.

[62] Grimm, 1857, 21, 25, 113. Grimm's anthology also contains many stories of magical facture such as the Elves and the Shoemaker.

marital fortune was culturally rich and variegated, the subject of myth and folklore, literary and oral storytelling traditions interfused.

Following the inaugural publication of Arabian fairy tales by Straparola, the first to include in print the distinctive cinder-girl was the Neapolitan poet-courtier and *accademico* Giovan Battista Basile in his *Pentamerone* (1634–6) or *Tale of Tales*.[63] Basile had travelled to Venice and Venetian-ruled Crete among other places in the Middle East, where he may have encountered Arabian-derived fairy tales as well as Straparola's collection. Purportedly written to amuse an expectant princess with comic stories of make-believe, Basile's *Tale of Tales* comprises a framing text of magical composition like the *Arabian Nights*, inset with forty-nine further fairy tales. Narrated by a succession of garrulous nursemaid storytellers over five days, like Straparola, these are interspersed with songs, games, and proverbial riddles. Situated in a courtly palace in the surrounds of Naples, Basile's stories are narrated in dialect with a piquant Neapolitan play on words indebted to the poetic embellishments of his Neapolitan compatriot Giambattista Marino's celebrated encomium of literary marvels. Each evening concludes with a comic eclogue devoted to prophetic objects or materialities of a courtier's fortune: a crucible that tests the truth of men; a dyer's cosmetic colours that conversely make wicked men appear good and good men evil; a woodstove whose quickly passing heat is a comic allegory of *vanitas*; and a proverbial hook for fishing fortunes at the bottom of a wishing well.

Basile's frame story is that of a displaced princess who reclaims her rightful position with the aid of three magical objects – a walnut, a chestnut, and a hazelnut, each housing tiny automata within – and her own enchanted powers of storytelling. Her literary persona recalls the Arabian princess Scheherazade, whose stories of wonder also comprised such magical objects as an ebony flying horse, a gold trumpeter, and a moving silver peacock. Other stories turn on female domestic objects such as metamorphic spindles and Pygmalion-like sugar-dolls or marzipan sculptures that come to life. These objects magically mirror the destinies of their owners: when the king of Lungapergola desires an heir, an enchanted recipe of sea-dragon stew causes the queen's cook to conceive as well as the queen herself along with all their chattels, in a comic profusion of baby beds, tables, chairs, chests, and even infant chamber pots.[64] In Basile, his Cinderella is magically clothed by her fairy-benefactor to rival the other girls' 'all fluttering, bedaubed and painted, all ribbons, bells and gewgaws, all flowers and perfumes, roses and posies'.[65] She travels on a white horse with a diamond bridle or in a golden carriage, and is dressed like a regal bride, such

---

[63] Basile, 1891; Magnanini 2008; Canepa, 1999.   [64] Basile, 1891, I:9.
[65] Basile,1932, I:6, 59.

that the story takes up themes of the wiles of love and marriage as female fortune. She also loses a slipper, though its material description is unspecified, here termed a *chianiello (pianella),* and the subject of Neapolitan folksong, as Benedetto Croce identified. In outdoing her stepsisters, Basile wittily concluded about life's metamorphic games of chance at the hands of *la fata* or fairy-fate: 'What madness to challenge the stars!'[66]

Perrault's *Tales* and those of his *salon* coterie were undoubtedly indebted to both Basile and Straparola, whose texts they evidently read together alongside recitations of their own literary oeuvres. Their readings also comprised the work of Perrault's friend and colleague in the Académie Royale des Inscriptions et Médailles, Antoine Galland. A celebrated Orientalist and bibliophile to a number of illustrious court patrons, culminating in his appointments to the royal library and Professor of Oriental Languages at the Collège Royale, Galland was both a linguist and archaeologist who travelled extensively in the Middle East on behalf of the Crown. As Colbert's appointed translator for the French East India Company, centred on the Middle East, he was also an indefatigable collector of Arabic manuscripts and inscriptions for the royal collections. Like Perrault, Galland worked at the fulcrum of the complex intersections of a globalising commerce and culture in the age of Louis. His travel diaries detail his daily examination and acquisition of proffered Oriental manuscripts. These included a Syrian fourteenth–fifteenth-century recension of fairy tales he bought in the 1690s, which he would subsequently translate and publish as *A Thousand and One Nights*, also comprising additional tales he collected from Arabic oral storytelling traditions.[67] If subsequent nineteenth-century scholarship on the *Arabian Nights* was critical of Galland's beautifully jewelled rendition of these tales, it yet acknowledged his pivotal position not only to the proliferation of the Indo-Persian fairy tale but also to broader cultures of early modern 'orientalism'.[68] In addition to his extensive published translations of Persian and Arabic literature, including its tales of enchanted marvels, he was also author to many tracts on Arabic culture of an historical nature that testify to his particular position within royal patronage at the cultural crossroads of Colbert's globalising French economy: on the origins of chess, the ancient Egyptian trumpet, proverbial Arabic *bon mots*, and coffee.

Perrault's 1695 manuscript of the Mother Goose Tales (not yet including Cinderella) is dedicated to Mademoiselle, the king's niece Elizabeth-Charlotte d'Orléans, then nineteen years old and the highest-ranking unmarried princess

---

[66] Basile, 1891, I:6, I, 84, 86, and note 35 on her slipper.
[67] Galland published *Les mille et une nuit* in a succession of volumes from 1704 to 1717. Bauden & Waller, 2020; Horta, 2017; Makdisi & Nussbaum, 2008.
[68] Dew, 2009.

Figure 12 Charles Perrault, *Mother Goose Tales,* mss Pierpont Morgan Library, 1695, frontispiece (Photo: Pierpont Morgan Library).

in France. In the frontispiece illustration, the spinning nursemaid is the fount of fairy tales for her young charges gathered round her (**Fig. 12**).[69] As an offering for Madamoiselle's amusement, and surely of Perrault's patronage, the epithet of the broody Mother Goose is on the one hand folkloric, on the other royalist in its dedication. For, the fabled Mother Goose was further configured through the

---

[69] www.themorgan.org/collection/charles-perrault/manuscript (last accessed 2021); Marin, 1990.

recollection of a mythic medieval French Queen Pédauque or *pieds-d'oie*, goose-footed as the sign of a plentiful maternal care. A popular soubriquet of French queenship, Queen Pédauque was also known for her mythic ability to spin a story so that straw became metaphorical gold. She was remembered as the 'homespun' people's queen whose kind words made her the protectress of her flock. Among Aesop's antique *Fables* was that of the Goose that laid golden eggs, a cross between a cautionary tale of counting your blessings and a sumptuary admonishment against over-reaching yourself in the pursuit of riches. In the retelling by Perrault's fellow academician, the court poet Jean de La Fontaine, the story became 'The Goose with the Golden Eggs', a gentle counterpoint of anecdotal plenty like the 'Mother Goose' appellation for good storytelling.[70] Hence, Mother Goose became the nursemaid-protector of children and family in the name of the queens of France, spinning her stories from the cloth of culture, both of folklore and majesty.

The conceit of the nursemaid spinning yarns is also manifest in the printed frontispieces to d'Aulnoy's multi-volume fairy tales published in 1697 (**Fig. 13**), the same year as Perrault's *Mother Goose Tales*.[71] D'Aulnoy's opening illustrations variously depict a young woman reading to a group of children from a book, or a woman unwrapping a ball of wool, like Straparola's Clotho, to suggest the myriad tales she will tell for the children in her care. The idea of the story's thread was also emblematised in the painted metal sculptures after Aesop's *Fables* for the garden labyrinth at Versailles, orchestrated by Perrault for the young Dauphin. The entrance to the labyrinth opened with a *putto* holding a ball of yarn, as the means to find the way through the maze and so to the artefact-collection of stories it represented.[72] Also royalist in cast, d'Aulnoy's corpus is dedicated to Madame, the wife of Philippe d'Orléans and sister-in-law to Louis XIV, Elizabeth-Charlotte de Bavière, in the name of fairy-queens who govern the kingdom with their words of spun gold. D'Aulnoy's literary endeavours arising from her social and cultural position as host to a celebrated Parisian *salon*, she wrote historical novels as well as collections of fairy tales. Herself the victim of a young and disastrous arranged marriage, which had forced her into some twenty years of exile, d'Aulnoy dedicated her fairy tales to '*les dames*' surely in tacit acknowledgement of her *salon* coterie, like Perrault's

---

[70] La Fontaine, 1668, V:13; Armstrong, 1944.

[71] D'Aulnoy's 1697 *Contes des fées* was published in a close succession of imprints also comprising a four-volume 1698 edition (though bound as two) and a three-volume series, *Contes galans, dedié au dames*, published in 1696 (in which her *Cinderella* appears) with a second volume, *Contes nouveau, ou les fées à la mode*, and *Cabinet des Contes* in 1698; Hannon, 1998; Cagnat-Deboeuf, 2008; Bloom, 2022.

[72] Perrault, 1679.

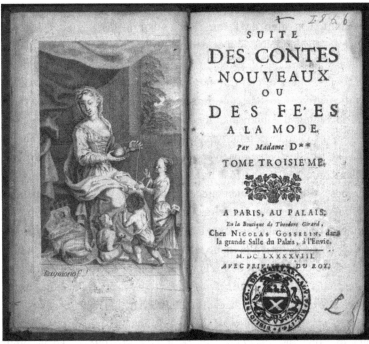

Figure 13 Marie-Catherine le Jumel de Barneville, Baroness d'Aulnoy, *Contes*, 1698, frontispieces, Bibliothèque National de France (Photo: Gallica).

Apology, and of her great literary forebear at the early fifteenth-century French court, Christine de Pizan. The author of *The City of Ladies*, de Pizan wrote allegorically of the leading place of women in the fabric of civil society and in justification of women's education, and remained an exalted French figure of court literary patronage in the name of women.[73]

Over the period 1696–8, a close succession of *salon* fairy tales by a range of authors, including d'Aulnoy and Perrault, appeared from Parisian presses, notably that of Claude Barbin, who would also publish Galland's *Thousand and One Nights*. Clearly the closely-woven offshoot of an efflorescent vogue for such tales composed in the first instance for evening entertainments in the *salons*, these stories were then prepared for press as a newly fashionable genre of literary endeavour. L'Héritier de Villandon published her 1696 miscellany comprising fairy tales similar to d'Aulnoy's in which the author introduced her work as a genre then à la mode within the *salons* circles they frequented. Charlotte-Rose de Caumont de La Force published her *Tales of Tales* (1697); Chevalier Louis de Mailly, *Illustrious Fairies* (1698); Henriette-Julie Castelnau de Murat, *Fairy Tales* (1698); and Jean de Prechac, his humorous pastiche on the genre, *Contes moins contes que les autres*, liberally punning on the double meaning of 'conte' as *Tales Less Silly Than the Rest* (1698).[74] Their commentary, in their texts as in their correspondence and memoirs, indicates that the fashion for the fairy tale in the closing decade of the seventeenth century also comprised their historical consideration, particularly the widely translated and much-read Straparola. Like Straparola's concluding riddles, Perrault also closed each story with a sequence of moralising verses that playfully elaborated both a lesson in virtue and one in courtly advancement. For *Cinderella*, Perrault's moral lesson was first of good grace and, then, satirically, of good patronage at court, in the figure of the fateful 'fairy' godmother.[75] Within the Parisian *salons*, much of the fairy tale's humour turned on such witty social parody, albeit in the light allegory of fairy-fate. Howsoever veiled in the semblance of magic, the stories were as much concerned with the present fates of political fortune, marital alliance, and inheritance as with their literary antecedents.

D'Aulnoy's *Contes* is generally recognised as the first published usage of the term fairy tale, as *contes des fées*. Titling them *Fashionable Fairies* or *Collection-Cabinets of Tales* (as also those of La Force, de Mailly, and L'Héritier de Villandon) her volumes declared themselves variously as collections-cabinets of stories, seemingly housing the magical objects within.

---

[73] Adams, 2014.

[74] La Force, 1697; L'Héritier de Villandon, 1696; Mailly, 1698; Murat, 1698, Prechac, 1698. On Barbin, Reed, 1974.

[75] Perrault, 1981, 177–8.

D'Aulnoy's stories are suffused with references to princely collections of art and *objets d'art*, comprising architecture, painting, and sculpture, as well as assemblies of precious materials and the artefactual treasuries that characterised royal cabinets. Among them, d'Aulnoy's lavish account of Cinderella is part Hansel and Gretel and a measure of Little Red Riding Hood. Studded with precious textiles of gold- and silver-thread, pearls, and diamonds, brocades and velvets, costly lace and ribbon, Cinderella's slipper, in d'Aulnoy's account, is of red-silk velvet embroidered with pearls, her dresses of gold and sky-blue satin, covered in diamonds as brilliant as the sun and the moon. Her skin is as white as snow, coloured with the vermilion of roses, her teeth like pearls, her lips of coral. D'Aulnoy's Cinderella is more beautiful than a Helen, herself jewel-like in the manner of Petrarchan poetic convention.[76] Hers is a fairy-tale luxury fit for a queen.

The thread of the story, like that of cloth, is itself a richly embroidered one in d'Aulnoy's telling. Her narratives are intricately woven with every kind of enchantment, of character as of plot, and studded with luxury detail. The fairy-tale genre, as it appears already in the texts of Straparola and Basile, and which would also configure Galland's *Arabian Nights*, was bespangled with precious objects of material and magical facture, with a rich nomenclature to describe them, nowhere more so than in matters of dress and textile. Basile begins his account with Cinderella's instruction in the art of embroidery as the needlework of queens, while her fall from grace is marked by a descent from silks to dish-clouts. In Perrault, the allusions are more lightly made, Cinderella's ball-dress of gold cloth set against her tattered cinder-rags. D'Aulnoy's story begins with the parents' misfortunes, also characterised in terms of textile wealth, losing their lace ruffs so that they must take up weaving fishing nets. Her more exuberant text is thick with textile details, from the skein of thread gifted to Cinderella by her fairy-godmother in order to find her way through the woods as an allegory of her destiny (and thus her story), to dresses of gold and silver so studded with gold and diamonds as to weigh, apparently, 1,000 pounds. In social practice too, as d'Aulnoy would have known herself, aristocratic and royal wedding dress was so heavy with jewels that young brides had to be supported by their handmaids, causing court commentators to quip that French princesses 'carried their fortunes on their backs'.[77]

As tales of fortune in marriage, the French *salon* fairy tale was host to similar descriptions of female dress in order to signify both beauty and wealth. These literary textiles are themselves like veritable treasuries of gold, silver, and

---

[76] D'Aulnoy, 2004, 452, 454–5.   [77] Arizzoli-Clémentel & Gorguet Ballesteros, 2009, 47–8; Marly, 1987, 99–100.

jewels, and the marker of regal luxury. This is most pronounced in Sleeping Beauty narratives, which Perrault was the first to so name. In Perrault's account, the fateful spindle is coupled with a shimmering cloth of embroidered gold and silver on which the prince, a hundred years later, will find the dormant princess. These jewelled textiles take their place within a fulsome range of fairy-tale objects, at once social and imaginary, intended to invoke marvelling wonder. Comprising seeming jewels and precious stones fabled for their brilliance as for their display in the form of flowers and boughs of fruit, d'Aulnoy's text glitters with diamond roses, sapphire violets, tulips of amethyst and opal, and rubies like cherries with emerald leaves, surely in imitation of Aladdin's jewelled orchard, and certainly of then-current court fashions.[78] Her fairy-tale palaces are similarly of diamond and crystal, furnished in gold, silver, ivory, ebony, and richly jewelled objects of fabulous luxury. Yet other d'Aulnoy artefacts are clearly enchanted: caskets housing magical miniature creatures, speaking portraits, or flying automata. What is distinctive in Perrault's glass slipper is the wondrous opposition of the material to its purpose as a dancing shoe. As glass congeals from liquid to solid it cannot balletically bend or stretch, it can only sparkle and 'fit'.

3 Luxury Materialities

3.1 Miniver

In Balzac's disquisition on Cinderella's slipper, intentionally or otherwise, he probed the historical relationship between luxury and imaginary objects that Anatole France would subsequently repose. While Balzac argued for historical interpretation, France instead postulated literature as the domain of the figurative. In France's reading, the brilliant impossibility of Perrault's fairy-tale glass slipper was the point. The 'Cinderella Affair' brought forth a flood of literary comment precisely because it framed the question of historical writing, as to probability and improbability, within a work of fiction. For Balzac, as a proclaimed historical novelist of 'social realism', literature's fictions succeed to the extent of their probability, into which the reader can, albeit fictively, 'enter in'. For France, the starry immateriality of the glass slipper set within a narrative that is otherwise about magical making, rather than fictitious objects as such, was the fabled masterstroke of Perrault's tale. Howsoever it is cast, the case of Cinderella's glass slipper playfully puzzles any analysis of Renaissance materialities, as this section concerns. In its juxtaposition of social artefacts and fairy tales' impossible objects, as also of confectioned metaphors within the cultural

---

[78] D'Aulnoy, 2004, 308, 331; Arizzoli-Clémentel & Gorguet Ballesteros, 2009, 217.

imaginaries of figured speech, this section turns to the doubled 'production' of fairy-tale artefacts, in both material and fictional form.

To pose again Balzac's question as to *verre* or *vair*, glass or fur, within a history of Renaissance materialities both were prized and precious. Their respective histories constitute a cultural mirror of luxury consumption for the period. *Cristallo* glass production was the very recent achievement of the French Crown. Secreted by Colbert through a mixture of science and diplomacy from the vaunted Venetian workshops that had led the luxury manufacture of this lightsome and ethereal material for several centuries, it was institutionalised in France only with the Royal Manufactory for Mirror Glass in 1665, at first in the Parisian Faubourg St Antoine and Tourlaville in Normandy, and subsequently at St Gobain in Picardy from 1692.[79] Fur, by contrast, was the luxury product of global trade, to the Baltic and thence to Russian Siberia, and the remote Canadian forest. What the *coureur des bois* brought to the Canadian wilderness in exchange for the precious fur they sought was European wampum – tinctured glass beads and tiny mirrors from Murano – as valuable artefacts of myriad light reflection indeed conceived as an impossible materiality to the native hunters with whom they traded.[80] Glass-bead *conterie* were also used for trade across Africa, for ivory, jewels, gold, and slaves. Within a European trading economy, it is also the case that, throughout the Middle Ages, fur, like cloth, was understood as an equivalent form of currency with gold. Thus, the seventeenth-century Russian diplomat Nicolai Spathary described the fleece of the Siberian sable as a form of Hellenic wealth whose trade would underwrite the fortunes of the Romanov dynasty:

> a beast full marvellous and prolific, and it is found nowhere else in the world but in northern Siberia . . . its beauty comes to it with the snow . . . . And this is the beast that the ancient Greeks and the Romans called the Golden Fleece, and for the sake of that fleece the Greek Argonauts sailed the Euxine [Black] Sea to seek it, as the historians tell us.[81]

As European furs were increasingly depleted due to the long medieval history of deforestation, traders turned to new sources further afield, prompted by and prompting sixteenth-century global exploration. The Renaissance trade in luxury goods may be said to have driven the competitive early modern mercantilism of the European crowns who sponsored voyages of discovery as a means of extending their commercial empires. In the domain of fur, pelts were at their

---

[79] Scoville, 2008; Bondue, 2010.

[80] Heidenreich & Ray, 1976; Trivellato, 2000. Depending on the quality of the pelt, a beaver skin was valued at between a half and a pound-weight of glass beads.

[81] Baddeley, 1919, II, 271; Richards, 2014.

fullest if hunted during the coldest months, as Spathary noted, and from the deep wintry landscapes of Siberia and the Canadian north, depending on native hunters for their procurement. Particularly prized were furs that whitened during winter as snow camouflage; these included the precious ermine pelt, and *vair* or *menuvair* – in English, miniver – the fur of the Baltic squirrel. While dark sable was most valued as the fur approached a lustrous glossy black tinged with gold, as its epithet of 'golden fleece' acknowledged, ermine and miniver were instead prized for their silky-white winter coats. In the case of miniver, the soft, milk-white underbelly might be juxtaposed with edging of the Baltic squirrel's silver-grey topcoat to produce pelts of variegated colouring as the historical etymology of '*vair*' was understood to convey. In winter, the grey took on a bluish cast that was especially valuable. When stitched together, the furs formed an arrangement of interlocking chevrons of blue on white. Miniver was used as a luxury lining to woollen garments in which the distinctive patterning was visible at the sleeves and trains, as also in collars, cloaks, and cuffs, as represented in Jan van Eyck's depiction of the Arnolfini bride to the Tuscan textile merchant-prince, the prosperity of their marriage also marked in the richly decorated glass mirror behind them (**Fig. 14**).[82] Ermine fur too might be stitched with a black contrast from the tip of the animal's tail, to produce a white pelt with distinctive black-striated tippets. This patterning of the sewn pelts would be variously reproduced within armorial design, as ermine tips on a white field, or as interlocking vair-bells of azure and white, further testament to the place of fur within a late medieval and Renaissance conception of sumptuary dress. In terms of footwear, fur was used to line boots and outer galoshes with decorative cuffs. Such a luxury shoe was the exclusive purview of wealth, for the costs were extravagant. At the opposite pole to court, tanned-hide footwear rudely stitched and laced with thongs was worn by labourers and peasants since time immemorial (**Fig. 15**). At all social levels, albeit of different kinds and composition, fur and fur-lined slippers were surely available. Yet, as Anatole France quipped in his bemused debate with Balzac, a princess in ballroom dress with fur dancing slippers was more likely a *comédie humaine*.

Glass, by contrast, was a manufactured material, howsoever ethereal and seemingly magical in its metamorphic making. Across Renaissance Europe, Murano remained the centre of the most highly prized luxury glass, which was, at the time, a commodity of value readily comparable with fur, sought after for its seemingly impossible airy fineness and jewel-like sparkle. It was particularly Murano's crystalline transparency that the French Crown sought to purloin and master in its establishment of a Royal Manufactory for luxury glass to rival Venice.

---

[82] Seidel, 1993, on the Arnolfini representation of material goods.

Figure 14 Jan van Eyck, *Arnolfini double portrait*, 1434, oil on oak panel,
National Gallery London (Photo: Wikimedia).

While Murano's production remained that of individually crafted blown-glass of
hand-held dimensions, French technology instead turned to the industrialised
production of glass-plate for full-length windows and mirrors. Fostered by
Colbert across the 1670s, this enabled a new interior decorative order of cast
and reflected light epitomised in the Hall of Mirrors at Versailles. The main
ingredients for glassmaking were by and large cheap and plentiful – crushed
stone or sand brought from the beaches, firewood for the furnaces, and ash made
from burning marsh plants or brushwood, so that the weighty cost of glass resided

Figure 15 Peter Breughel the Elder, *Peasant Wedding*, 1567, oil on wood panel,
Kunsthistorisches Museum Vienna (Photo: Wikimedia).

in the skill of its making, as Perrault, the administrator of its production, undoubtedly knew. Not the least of its marvellously metamorphic manufacture was the
transformation of humble and quotidian materials into palatial splendour. In the
words of James Howell, the seventeenth-century British glassmaker and visitor to
Murano, 'it being a rare kind of knowledge and chymistry to transmute dust and
sand (for they are the only main ingredients) to such a diaphanous pellucid dainty
body as you see a crystal-glass is', which he concluded with a playful elision
between crystal glasses and lasses.[83] Similarly, Cendrillon's name – in Italian
Cenerentola, in German Aschenputtel – springs from the ashes or cinders of the
hearth she swept, out of which her fairy-godmother would magically fashion her
glass slippers. Perrault's playful conceit of Cinderella's glass slipper surely arose
in an informed approximation of her sartorial refashioning to that of Louis' royal
glass-manufacturing for France. In a figurative microcosm of the Hall of Mirrors,
her glass slipper was made by a kind of artisanal and chemical magic from the
wood-ash collected by charcoal-burners and cinder-girls.

Alongside windows and mirrors, the French manufactory also enabled an
expanding production of small-scale glass decorative objects comparable to
contemporaneous developments in the history of porcelain. Similarly nurtured

---

[83] Howell, 1641, I, XXIX, 56.

Figure 16 Delftware ornamental slipper, dated 1697, The Metropolitan
Museum of Art (Photo: Metropolitan Museum of Art).

as a French manufacture in the closing years of the seventeenth century, the
subsequent development of white-paste porcelain would produce decorative
arts as well as dinnerware. In a parallel and certainly emulative history of their
facture, glass-paste was made in imitation of porcelain, known as *lattimo* or
milk-glass, while faience ceramics of fired quartz were close cousins. Together,
they produced an inter-related range of decorative objects for mantelpiece,
dining-, and dressing-table display. Among a burgeoning range of domestic
decorative artefacts in such materials, often for marriage gifts, finely wrought
ornamental 'slippers' were made as drinking cups for the ceremonial toasts,
containers for sugared almonds, or as dressing-table cases for betrothal jewellery (**Fig. 16**). Auguries of good fortune, the ornamental slipper was particularly
associated with marriage as the coupling of a pair, in a betrothal metaphor of
archaic origin, as Straparola's Lucrezia had narrated in comic vein. Among
decorative betrothal slippers, as nuptial drinking cups they might also be made
of glass.[84] Thus, in Perrault's *Cinderella*, the narrative of the slipper is surely

---

[84] There are further examples at Musée de la Céramique, Rouen, and Gardiner Museum of
Ceramics, Toronto. An example of a glass drinking flute in the form of a boot with etched
'lace' decoration on the hightop and glass 'spurs' is at the Musée National de la Renaissance,
Château Ecouen (Inv. No. ECL2037); there are also examples of medieval Persian drinking boots
in glass (Kofler Collection, LNS 110 KG), as evidence of Arabic equestrian dress as well as
decorative glassware in the form of footwear.

that of marriage magically elaborated as a fairy tale, in which the telling shoe is promissory, sought after, and, at last, reunited with its partner as a material allegory of betrothal.

3.2 Dictionaries

While Perrault wrote his fairy tales under the pseudonym of the rustic story-teller Mother Goose, he was, at the same time, a much-celebrated and prolific author on the leading debates of literary culture in his day. A founding member and secretary to Louis XIV's Académie Royale des Inscriptions et Médailles, and subsequently of its academic parent devoted to all aspects of the French language across the arts and sciences, the Académie Française, Perrault's literary career was staged at the centre of French cultures of humanist erudition in the age of Louis. At its inception, the Académie Royale des Inscriptions et Médailles was dedicated to the study of the monuments, documents, and languages of ancient cultures, and specifically concerned with the composition as well as transcription of classical epideictic inscriptions. These were used as *encomia* to the reign of Louis XIV on public monuments and medals in honour of the king as well as literary publications of the Academy. The Académie Française in those years was similarly engaged with producing the first diction-ary of the French language, whose preface Perrault would also write, dedicated to the king and published in 1694 as a concerted refinement and codification of a national lexicon. While Perrault published his *Tales* under the soubriquet of Mother Goose, in his contributions to the leading cultural and literary debates of the time he styled himself as 'M. Perrault de l'Académie Françoise'. Perrault's Academy texts were all dedicated to the collective glories of Louis' reign, of the king himself, but also the augmentation of learning and culture under his royal aegis, from his sagacious ministers to his brilliant men of letters, scientists, architects, painters, and musicians. Steeped in a classical humanist erudition, as his position within the Inscriptions et Médailles makes manifest, yet in the burning seventeenth-century *parallèle* (or, as it was wittily renamed, *querelle*) of ancients and moderns that he led, Perrault was the great advocate of the moderns. His polemic argued the case for the moderns as equal to the ancients in his comparison of the reign of Louis XIV with Augustus.[85] Perrault's Mother Goose, howsoever disguised as the homely folkloric 'spinner of yarns', in fact arose within the highest circles of humanist erudition of Louis XIV's '*grand siècle*'.

---

[85] Perrault, 1688; 1696; 1668 as an encomium to Le Brun; and his contribution to the Académie *Dictionnaire* – Perrault, 1694 – dedicated to the king.

Among Perrault's fairy tales was the often-told story of Griselda, one of love's travails on the part of the long-suffering shepherdess-princess taken from Boccaccio's *Decameron*, which would also configure painted imagery on Renaissance marriage-chests.[86] Perrault's rendition in praise of patience, written in verse and first declaimed at the Academy in 1691, was one with a by now extensive literary echo, from Petrarch to Chaucer and Christine de Pizan. As a work of both folklore and academic discourse, Perrault's Griselda manifests the richly interwoven literary fabric of his *Tales*, between the Academy, the *salon*, and the proverbial nursemaid. While Perrault's Griselda was first presented in recital to the Académie, his *Tales* were originally performed and written for the audience of the *salon*. As their extensive scholarship attests, the Parisian *salons* positioned themselves in a considered counterpoint to the court at Versailles, as a conversational culture combining comparative informality and refinement like that of Lucrezia's Venetian carnival villa. Thus, the *salon* was also distinct from, if in close social rapport with, the Academy, its dictionary, and its projected refinement of the French language. Here the French fairy tale, like its Italian predecessors, flourished as a genre of witty reflection on both noble mores and academic lexicons.

Though scholars have debated the precise historical origins of the term, whether within the early seventeenth-century *salons* themselves or subsequently through Molière's biting parody of them in his *Précieuses ridicules*, the women who led the art of wit and conversation seen to epitomise *salon* sociability and its literary manifestations would become known for a figurative literary preciosity.[87] The *précieuse* epithet, as manifest in the fairy tale, was at once literal and metaphorical, both complimentary and satirical, for these were stories studded with jewels in narrative and linguistic terms, undoubtedly in imitation of their Arabian forebears as well as the dazzling court culture of Versailles. This *salon* conception of the fairy tale as an embroidered or enamelled text bespangled with literary *jeux-de-mots* like so many jewels runs throughout. It is directly allegorised in Perrault's story of 'Les Fées', its title a double entendre of fairies and fateful acts, and another version of the Cinderella narrative fused with the biblical tale of Rebecca at the well. It was a narrative that Straparola had also used in the story of Biancabella with subsequent versions in many fairy-tale anthologies.[88] In Perrault's telling, two daughters are greeted by a poor stranger at a well, who asks for their assistance; the kind daughter helps the old woman (a fairy-godmother in disguise), while the other haughtily refuses. The first is gifted with the jewelled speech of a courtly *bienséance*, so that diamonds and pearls accompany her words just

---

[86] Perrault, 1981, 57–93; Baskins, 1991.   [87] Molière, 1660.   [88] Straparola, 1550, I III 3.

like a courtier, while the other (arguably also a courtier) speaks only the poisoned words of toads and vipers.[89] The purported literary ambition of *les précieuses*, close to the Academy's dictionary project, was similarly with the gem-like refinement of the French language in forging a French culture at once historical and modern. Throughout, there is a literary thematic of sparkle that pervades, of fairy-tale jewels as a metaphor of their textual splendour. For these were brilliantly surfaced texts in which the wit of wordplay was conceived as the literary equivalent of the gems in which fairy-tale princesses were dressed. The works abound with *calembours*, often of complex historical etymology suffused with neologisms and archaisms close to the literary cultures of the Academy's *Dictionary*, and also with a paronomasia of the Parisian *salon mondaine*. Apparently light-hearted in subject, yet of sparkling wit, the textual *equivoque* of the *Contes* was itself a 'parallel of ancients and moderns', punning liberally on French à la mode alongside the canons of ancient literature, Louis' court, and national history, in equal measure. Their textual sparkle is brilliantly emblematised in Perrault's magisterial glass slipper.

When Balzac raised the issue of 'mistranslation' in the matter of Cinderella's slipper, as to *verre* or *vair*, his commentary concerned the historical etymology of a word that was already by his day archaic, though current in Perrault's time. Whether historical or typographical, whether intentionally or otherwise, Balzac surely also touched on a further elaboration of Perrault's 'quarrel of ancients and moderns' regarding the question of translation itself. In seventeenth-century French literature, the translation debate crystallised around the academician Nicolas Perrot d'Ablancourt (and his critics such as Gilles Ménage). As the author of etymological dictionaries and his 1650 *Origins of the French Language*, d'Ablancourt wrote in a considered counterpoint to scientific figures such as Pierre-Daniel Huet, also an academician. Huet's 1683 *On the Best Mode of Translation* made the case for literal accuracy above all else, while d'Ablancourt's prefaces to his translations of Julius Caesar, Lucian, Tacitus, and Minucius Felix, among others, conversely argued in favour of modernising adaption in matters of translation. The debate was characterised as Huet's word-for-word method, as against what Ménage would term d'Ablancourt's *belles infidèles*, like a beautiful if unfaithful lover, seductive but untrustworthy.[90]

It was a debate rich in classical antecedents itself, within the discussion of Latin translations of Greek texts by figures such as Cicero, Quintilian, and Horace, whose authority was insistently cited in Renaissance elaborations of the question. As much scholarship has recognised, the issue was critical to the great

---

[89] Perrault, 1981, 163–7.   [90] d'Ablancourt, 1650; Huet,1683; Zuber, 1968.

humanist history of translation undertaken by figures such as Leonardo Bruni and Lorenzo Valla in the vast fifteenth-century rendering of ancient Greek texts into Latin. Within the debate lay the recognition that literal fidelity could belie literary form. Bruni's *On Correct Interpretation* recognised the question of how to render different linguistic effects or styles in translation, from Cicero's *copia* to Sallust's plain style. Valla's historical philology instead famously led him to decry the Donation of Constantine as a forgery on the basis of anachronism, turning on a single word.[91] This is lightly allegorised in Straparola's recourse to various languages and dialects, as also in Venetian Renaissance texts of polyglossia such as the *The Dream of Poliphili* of 1499. *Mot-à-mot* to *belles infidèles*, the historical course of the question was rich and complex within the humanist project of translation, which would comprise the weighty texts of Plato and Euclid alongside Galland's fairy-tale rendition of *One Thousand and One Nights*. As academician of both classical inscriptions and the French language, howsoever the recourse to the folkloric Mother Goose as the purported author of his fairy tales, Perrault undoubtedly wrote in full knowledge of the cultural weight of language and its permutations in the hands of translation.

3.3 Verre-vair-vert

Among the infinite challenges in translating from Greek into Latin, as Perrault surely knew, was that of colour. As Johann Wolfgang von Goethe and subsequently William Gladstone would later argue, the ancient Greek literary lexicon is obscure in the differentiation of colour, instead distinguishing the visual effects of, for example, landscapes and the elements through a vocabulary of light.[92] Latin, by contrast, offered a full spectrum of terminology for colour derived from the materials of which their pigments were made. Within the broad cultural matrix of a Plinian *Natural History*, colour's dyes – used for textiles as for paints and other artefacts including glass, mosaic, enamels, and porcelain – were conceived as the product of the plants and minerals by which they were made. This titular identification of colour's effects with the materialities of its making would also shape the late medieval imaginary of heraldic colour, as Michel Pastoureau has brilliantly argued.[93] In the distinctive clarity of its highly restricted palette, heraldry deployed only six colours, with the sometime addition of imperial *purpure* procured from the prized Tyrian sea mollusc. In addition to *argent* (white or silver), *or* (yellow or gold), sable (black, like the fur), and *azur* (blue, derived from lapis lazuli) were *gules* (red as in sanguine and genus for bloodlines and lineage), and *vert* (green or *viridium*, as in verdigris).

---

[91] Botley, 2004.   [92] Goethe, 1810; Gladstone, 1858, 3, 458–99.
[93] Pastoureau, 2013; and his larger series of books on colours. On green, see also Smith, 2009.

Verdigris, the oxidation residue of brass and copper, produced a brilliant but highly unstable green; while finely ground malachite, itself a copper ore in crystalline form, and which was mined together with the metal, yielded bright but costly green pigments. By far the majority of green dye was plant-based. Fern, plantain, oak, nettle, as well as certain barks produced plentiful earthen or grey-green shades, though few were easily stabilised. A stronger green from plant dyes came from superimposing yellow weld onto blue woad to produce a mixed colour of variable hue.

Like glass, in its varied colouring from thick workaday bottle green to ethereal *cristallo*, green dyes ranged across the social spectrum. Hence, green became the colour of fortune, in life as in love. As the chivalric figure of the Green Knight makes manifest, green was the colour of love's pursuit, of woods and meadows, and so of verdant spring in a calendar metamorphosis of the seasons within a medieval imaginary. '*Vert galant*' was the month of May, youth, and courtship, but also the rustic, for the right of *vert* comprised the terms of medieval forest law and so of the royal hunt. Its arboreal greenery was the forester's shelter and thus a folkloric imaginary of spring's leafy return within the cycle of the seasons. Similarly, the fairy's magic wand that transformed Cinderella's rustic pumpkin into a carriage, through the mediation of the medieval *grimoires* or books of spells, intimated a greenwood bough. Overladen with the Homeric caduceus of vicarious fate that made Odysseus alternately old and then young again in the watchful hands of Athena, it was also an intimation of Joseph's miraculously flowering biblical rod. As Perrault, man of the *Dictionary*, undoubtedly knew, the etymology of *vert* was from the Latin *vertere*, meaning to turn. Its linguistic cascade comprised both the agrarian turn of the plough in furrows as the augury of spring's plentiful promise, and the calligraphic return of the pen in the composition of verse, but also the sugges-tion of fate's changeable prospect in matters of fortune and of love. In a manuscript illustration to Christine de Pizan's *Book of Fortune*, Fortuna bears a green and golden-yellow robe to signify the changeability of fate, while her brothers are dressed in green and grey respectively, as emblems of *eur* or happy chance, and *meseur* as mischance (**Fig. 17**).

As the emblem of ardent spring-times and so of fickle fortune, green was also the colour of envy and melancholy. Thus the ballad of Lady Greensleeves long attributed to Henry VIII is a song of lost love as changeable as the colour, while Shakespeare's Iago would name jealousy 'the green-eyed monster which doth mock the meat it feeds on'. *As You Like It*'s 'Under the Greenwood Tree' is also a song of changeable fortune like the seasons, in the woodlands of courtly exile's 'winter and rough weather' as Perrault himself would later know. As in medieval ballads of Robin Hood, the forest's merry men are in and out of

Figure 17 Christine de Pizan, *Livre de la mutacion de Fortune*, mss 1403, Musée Condé Chantilly (Photo: Réunion des Musées Nationaux).

fortune, clothed in green like the *vert* of the woods in which they shelter.[94] In a folkloric vein, the French nursery rhyme of the little green mouse is a pet and emblem of spring as changeable as her colour, *coquine*. Hence, in Jan van Eyck's Arnolfini wedding portrait, the betrothed is dressed in an abundantly draped vivid green wool richly lined with ermine **(Fig. 14)**.[95] In Peter Breughel the Elder's *Peasant Wedding*, the bride is also clothed in green set against a deep green ceremonial cloth of marriage from which her paper crown, as a Cinderella-queen for the day, is suspended, while she bears a cloth tiara of red and gold **(Fig. 15)**.[96]

From the providence of love to those of family estate, green was also the colour of fortunes won and lost in finance and trade, in life as in ships at sea.

---

[94] Shakespeare, 1623, *Othello*, 3.3.170; *As You Like It*, 2.5.   [95] Seidel, 1993.
[96] Sullivan, 1994.

Figure 18 Quentin Metsys, *De wisselaer*, 1514, oil on wood panel, Musée du Louvre Paris (Photo: Wikimedia).

Thus, in Quentin Metsys' *De wisselaer* (1514), the moneychanger and his wife sit together at a table covered with green woollen baize on which he practises his trade of testing and weighing gold. The measure of character in the face of fate, his fortunes are further reflected in the small silvered blown-glass mirror before him (**Fig. 18**).[97] The gold he measures is the currency of fortune, while the green felted wool is its sign. With the rise of playing cards and billiards as games of chance during the Renaissance, durable baize became the conventional fabric of their table coverings. Green was the sign of changeable fortunes won and lost in games, in love and in life. Green baize would become the door covering to the servants' quarters in the prosperous eighteenth-century household, so marking the threshold between chance and mischance. It also undergirds the historic euphemism of the American dollar as 'greenback' for money and wealth. Close to Perrault, La Fontaine's fable of the bat, the bush, and the duck who lose their

---

[97] Kühn, 2015.

fortunes in a ship that founders at sea are now '*prêts à porter le bonnet vert*' to signify their declaration of bankruptcy, for the abundant plant dyes that made green so plentiful also charged it the colour of poverty.[98] While d'Aulnoy's jewelled Cendron wore royal red velvet slippers embroidered with pearls, Perrault's much gentler parody of marriage as fortune merely touched on the matter, through the brilliant phonic elision of *verre*, *vair*, and *vert*, and the material recollection of glassmaking's metamorphic manufacture of cinders into the glittering splendours of Versailles. Perrault's masterstroke was to render Cinderella's dancing shoe from a precious crystalline glass that might also become rich fur or fortune's ever-changeable green.

4 Fairy-Tale Objects

4.1 The Slipper

In d'Aulnoy's 1697 *Fairies à la Mode*, exactly contemporaneous with Perrault's *Mother Goose Tales*, this author of the *salon* styled her cinder-girl as Finette Cendron, so-named for her finesse in the comedic possession of a fine ear. The author wittily explains she was remarkable among her sisters for the ability to overhear precisely those conversations that could overturn or determine her fate and thus to subvert them, around which d'Aulnoy's more complex narrative turns. Finette's name encapsulates the lexical play of language that suffuses the *salon* fairy tales, in which its characters and their artefactual attributes are wrapped. As this section denominates, through a detailed study of the objects that figure Cinderella's fairy-tale destiny, each one is a magically materialist allegory of her fate.

In d'Aulnoy's telling, Finette's sisters' names are those of troubadour verses, Fleur d'Amour and Belle-de-nuit. But it is Cendron's cinder-girl name that lights the prince and his court afire, in a linguistic twist of her mysterious disappearances. *S'en vont, ainsi font*, in the children's rhyme of fifteenth-century marionette-dolls that disappear no sooner than they appear, is here-transformed into a parody of courtly speech and aristocratic *amour*:

> There was not a lover who would not leave his mistress for Cendron, not a poet who would not write in verse of Cendron; never did such a common name garner such acclaim in so short a time; it echoed incessantly in praise of Cendron; one had not eyes enough with which to look upon her, nor voice enough to praise her.[99]

In d'Aulnoy's account, Finette's godmother is *la fée Merluche*, like the *merlucciidae* fish, whose fortunes will also prosper in the hands of her immensely talented progeny. In both d'Aulnoy and Perrault, the fairy-benefactor of Basile's account is transformed into the social figure of the godmother – *la marraine* – so

---

[98] La Fontaine, 1668, XII:7. [99] D'Aulnoy, 2004, 452.

playfully invoking the character of court patronage in the double entendre of the queen – *ma reine* – which Cendron will herself become. In Perrault, her magic is wrought by means of a sceptre-like wand, so invoking the sign of regal power which will also become the instrument of her marriage – *bague/tte* – in a further playful elision with the wedding ring (as of the *salon* fairy-tale bagatelle). Inset within the fictions of fairy tales are myriad references to the social world of their *salon* composition – fashionable taffeta beauty-spot *mouches* from *la bonne Faiseuse* (surely also a pun on their facture), almond *dragées* and tarts from the *pâtissier* Le Coq, or roast partridge from the *rôtisseurs* Les Guerbois, as further witticisms on sweets and cockerels, and partridges out of the woods.[100] In d'Aulnoy, Finette tricks the ogres intent on eating the sisters with a ruthless deception. In her account, this is the means by which she acquires her cinder-girl epithet. As the ogre whets his appetite, in a Rabelaisian detail of *gargantua* as a folkloric grotesque of want, he devours 100 lambs and 100 suckling pigs, to Finette's horror, for he eats children like eggs. First pushing the ogre into his own oven to reduce him to cinders, she then dresses the hair of the ogress while promising her a king or a marquis in marriage before beheading her. Similarly, her sisters, dressed in their finest clothes, are assured they will marry rich (if untitled) financiers, who will be very pleased to marry penniless princesses.[101] As to her slipper, in d'Aulnoy's account it is a mule. In parodic explanation of its easy loss, her mule-slipper is like the little Spanish horse with a diamond-studded bridle that Finette rides, who kneels down before her so that she may mount him. In d'Aulnoy's further elaboration, the disconsolate prince finds Finette's 'doll-like mule' when he is out hunting, and as the king's heralds proclaim, he will marry only the foot that fits. Surely also a double entendre, all the girls and women of the kingdom seek to 'shoe the little horse'.

A hybrid animal known from archaic antiquity as a royal mount, the mule was bred across the Mediterranean throughout the Renaissance, for baggage trains as well as dainty equestrian horses. Mules carried the burden of luxury materials for trade across the early modern globe. 'Mule' was also, however, within an antique etymology the *mulleus calceus* or red shoe of the highest rank of Roman magistrate, as d'Aulnoy and her audience undoubtedly knew, then à la mode at the court of Louis XIV for both men and women. At court, the mule, like the mount, was often the outer-shoe or carrier of the jewelled slipper within it. D'Aulnoy's Cendron was a fairy tale of catachrestic comedy.

At the Palais-Royal on 24 October 1697, the year in which Perrault and d'Aulnoy's *Contes* first appeared, the Royal Academy of Music staged a

---

[100] Perrault, 1981, 172; D'Aulnoy, 2004, 280, 415. On the *'faiseuses de mouches'*, Thépaut-Cabasset, 2017.

[101] D'Aulnoy, 2004, 450.

ballet-opera titled *Europe Galante*, on the wiles of love as a sweet contest of nations – French, Spanish, Italian, and Turkish – the verses by Antoine Houdar de la Motte set to music byAndré Campra. Venus and Discord wage mock battle in which Venus triumphs as the patron of marriage, a courtly metaphor for those royal alliances that weddings could forge. In her 'literary forge' the dulcet sounds of grace, pleasure, and laughter ring out in fabricating the traits of love, interrupted by a symphony of discord, which Venus will quell through the ballet's *divertissements*.[102] Courtly opera-ballet's thematic orchestration of love as a series of witty entertainments was also performed at royal weddings. These were often staged in gracious acknowledgement of the bride, as with the *comédie-ballet*, the *Princesse of Navarre*, for the marriage of Maria Teresa to the Dauphin Louis, by Voltaire and Jean-Philippe Rameau on 23 February 1745 at Versailles.[103] Such entertainments brought together music, sung verse, or *recitar cantando*, with elaborate sets and costumes, comprising solo performances and *enfilade-entrées* of thematically orchestrated choreographies for a *corps de ballet*, often concluding with general dancing of audience and performers, also in emulation of Venetian carnival *divertimenti*. Among the many ballets of Louis' reign was also a *Psyche* staged on 16 January 1656, danced by the king in the part of gallant Springtime, and performed again with a play of the same name by Molière and Pierre Corneille in 1671 before Louis at the Tuileries Palace. Set within the great Salle des Machines or theatre of the Tuileries, the scenographies for the 1671 production were by Carlo Vigarani with music by Jean-Baptiste Lully to verses by Philippe Quinault, and further interspersed with balletic interludes by the court ballet-master and choreographer, Pierre Beauchamp. Following the Apuleian tale of changing fortune that is also Cinderella's, this Psyche is alternately abandoned in the wilderness, or welcomed into a golden palace with lush gardens of bowers and flowers made by fairies. Among the succession of balletic *entrées* on the theme of love blown by the four winds, including Apollo, Bacchus, and the Muses, are also the 'Arts' dressed as gallants, as the artisan-fabricators of Louis' court fêtes in fancy dress.[104]

Described in terms of marvelling wonder in letters, diaries, court correspondence, and newsletters, Louis' fêtes were occasions composed of every kind of luxury manufacture of the arts, from culinary delicacies to scenographic ensembles and costume dress, as of theatre, opera, and ballet. Set within the palace gardens of Versailles, their themes were as much pastoral as mythological, weaving together the figurative idioms of classical and romance literatures in the fabrication of scenographic illusions of Arcadian woods and enchanted islands. Guests were at once the social figures of Louis' court and the various

---

[102] Motte, 1697, 1–5. [103] Voltaire, 1745. [104] Benserade & Lully, 1671.

costume disguises in which they came. Their masks comprised shepherdess-princesses or dancing rustics reciting pastoral song, classical gods or foreign princes in balletic displays of exotic costume, and representations of the 'mechanical' arts that fabricated these entertainments in the so-named *Ballets of the Arts*. At a fancy-dress ball for the carnival of 1706, Louis' grandson the Duke of Burgundy, a great patron of court ballet and masquerade, came disguised as a lampstand with a candelabra headdress in silver and gilt, to represent the decorative arts and artisanal manufactures in costume. In the manner of *Europe galante*, such entertainments turned on the wit of their own illusion, playing at the threshold of luxury artistic manufacture and fairy-tale enchantment.[105]

Throughout d'Aulnoy's richly decorated fairy tales, her textual descriptions emulate the scenery and costume of court ballet, theatre, and the lavish fancy-dress garden fêtes of Louis' reign. A succession of scenic interludes of delightful contrasts between the courtly and the rustic, d'Aulnoy's recollection of Louis' court entertainments is surely in homage to the king but also a means of situating her stories in the minds of her audience within the cultural scenographies of Versailles. D'Aulnoy's princess Discrète is given a book of the newly fashionable metamorphic tale of Apuleius, as retold by La Fontaine in his *Loves of Psyche and Cupid* (1669), now set within the gardens of Versailles. Princess Discrète is an Apuleian Psyche herself, attended by Cupid and courted by a prince she may never look upon; to woo her, d'Aulnoy's invisible prince orchestrates magnificent balls and fêtes interspersed with the finest comedies of Corneille and Molière.[106] D'Aulnoy's story of Princess Gracieuse and Prince Percinet touches directly on Lully's *Psyche* for Louis, whose opera-ballet Gracieuse attends, in a literary acknowledgement of the 'play-within-the-play' as a soubriquet for d'Aulnoy's own. Like the Psyche of Apuleius, and fairy-tale princesses in general, Gracieuse is subject to the dramatic reversals of fortune that characterise her ascension from maiden to bride and queen. The wicked stepmother, grumpy Duchess Grognon, orders her abandonment in a forest with lions, bears, tigers, and wolves, where, in the utmost despair, she calls out to Percinet. At once, like a theatrical scene-change, the forest is transformed into a magnificent illumination culminating in the prospect of a crystal palace so brilliant it shines like the sun. Prince Percinet appears to her like the beautiful youth Cupid of the Apuleian tale of Psyche, dressed in green as the colour of his love for Gracieuse, to invite her into the Fairy Palace ruled by his mother the Queen of the Fairies. Together, they mount into a gilded sleigh pulled by two deer, in which they travel about the forest. Redolent of

---

[105] Marly, 1987, 61–79, 120; Milovanovic & Maral, 2009.
[106] D'Aulnoy, 2004, 585; La Fontaine, 1669.

Louis' pastoral scenographies for the garden fêtes at Versailles, they come upon shepherds and shepherdesses dressed *en galant* and dancing to the music of reeds and pipes; or villagers with their sweethearts singing and feasting by fountains. Percinet compliments Gracieuse that it is her presence which has transformed the forest into a place of courtly pleasures and amusements. Entering the palace to the sound of music, they then proceed into a great hall of crystal where Percinet has engraved the narrative of her life 'as if to rival Phidias'. After banqueting, they enter a *salon* splendidly decorated with gold and paintings to watch Lully's opera, the *Loves of Psyche and Cupid*, in which the player-shepherds sing directly to Gracieuse of her beauty, so weaving together the magnificent fictions of Louis' stage and d'Aulnoy's fairy tale as parallel courtly realms of illusion and enchantment. In the manner of a royal bride, Gracieuse is then dressed by the fairy-tale *couturiers* of her prince, who bear gifts of gowns in all colours set with embroidered jewels, lace, ribbons, gloves, and silk stockings, and a silver-gilt toilet service of ornamental chasing as would befit a queen's nuptials.[107] Throughout d'Aulnoy's fairy tales, her princes and princesses join in the courtly ballets that particularly distinguished Louis' entertainments at Versailles: the stately *pavanne*, with its long textile trains of the court dress; the quick-footed *bourées*, *sarabandes*, and *passe-pieds*; or the *danse ronde*.[108]

Across his reign, Louis worked closely with the designers for his *ballets d'entrées*, both of costumes and of sets, as with Benserade for the verses, and Lully as composer of the music. Louis himself appeared in some eighty court ballets across his reign; he also took daily dancing lessons with Pierre Beauchamp as his appointed director of the Royal Academy for Dance, which was formed in 1661. Here, Beauchamp would develop an increasing technical codification of the balletic steps later recorded by his successor, Pierre Rameau, in his illustrated manual of dance of 1725 **(Fig. 19)**.[109] Among its many recommendations as to the balletic etiquette of a royal ball and the five positions of the feet was the proper design of the dancing slipper: that it be suitably light and supple in order to accommodate the fine footwork it was intended to display.

Louis' own balletic performance was inaugurated in the role of Apollo, at fourteen years old, staged at the (no longer extant) Salle du Petit-Bourbon, with music by Lully and others, and verses by Benserade. As the Ballet Royale de la Nuit, it was staged from dusk to dawn, orchestrated as four thematically orchestrated night-watches on the pleasantries of courtly love and the playful pleasures of its *divertissements*. Henri de Gissey is generally thought to have designed the costumes, the drawings for which remain, depicting Louis in

---

[107] D'Aulnoy, 2004, 160–4.   [108] D'Aulnoy, 2004, 218, 228, 365, 582, 591.
[109] Rameau, 1725; Harris-Warrick & Marsh, 1994.

Figure 19 Pierre Rameau, *Le maître à danser*, 1725, Bibliothèque Nationale de France (Photo: Gallica).

cloth-of-gold embellished by jewels and figurations of the sun, while his skirt, sleeves, neck, and headdress are represented as solar rays surmounted by a crown of feathers. His shoes are of gold cloth with an arabesque heel, with an elaborately-jewelled sun devise, as also the garter to his hose (**Fig. 20**).[110]

---

[110] Benserade, 1653. The costume drawings for the ballet are preserved at the Bibliothèque de l'Institut de France (ms 1004), and Waddesdon Manor, Burdon & Thorpe, 2010.

Figure 20 Henri de Gissey, attrib., Louis XIV as Apollo, Ballet Royale de la Nuit 1653, Bibliothèque Nationale de France (Photo: Gallica).

His costume surely surpassed those of his accompanying dancers, as those remaining from the wardrobe for royal entertainments suggest cloth encrusted and bespangled with gold and silver-thread embroidery to effect a scintillating splendour of exquisite luxury (**Fig. 21**).[111]

If not of glass, yet the fine craftsmanship of shoes at the court of Louis XIV was a source of wonder and also parody. The seventeenth-century decorated court shoe flourished above all in men's dress, patronised by the king himself, while those of women followed suit, if generally occluded by the cascading length of their gowns (**Figs. 22** and **23**). Slippers of soft

---

[111] Gorce, 2009.

Figure 21 Dance costume, seventeenth century, gold and silver thread
embroidery with gold spangles, Musée de l'Opéra Paris
(Photo: Gallica Bibliothèque Nationale de France).

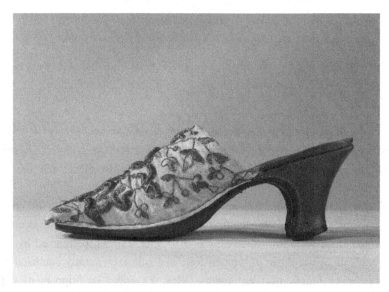

Figure 22 Mule slippers, c. 1660 English, kidskin and silk with floral
embroidery in silk and silver-gilt thread, Victoria & Albert Museum
(Photo: Victoria & Albert Museum).

Figure 23 Gold-silk latchet-tie shoes c. 1730, Paget Wade Collection, Berrington Hall Herefordshire (Photo: National Trust).

leathers and, above all, silk or velvet textiles in every colour, they were stitched with gold- and silver-metallic threads, embroidered and set with jewels, fringed with lace and tied with elaborate ribbons, jewelled buckles, frilled shoe-roses, or pompoms.[112] In the 1599 court portrait of Elizabeth I commissioned by her close associate Bess of Hardwick for her familial manor house at Hardwick Hall, the queen appears in a dress lavished with jewels and embroidery apparently stitched by Bess herself as a demonstration of her own needlework in emulation of Elizabeth's royal example (**Fig. 24**).[113] Here, the balletic slippers are visible at the foot of her gown, of white silk encrusted with gold thread, drop-pearls, and small garnet-like stones, whether of gems or glass, for Bess also owned a glassworks with which she famously outfitted the myriad diamond-pane windows of her stately home, like a veritable Aladdin's palace. In Henri Testelin's 1668 portrait of Louis XIV as patron of the Royal Academy for Painting and Sculpture, he is depicted in the full regalia of king as protector of the arts, bearing the gold sceptre of Charlemagne. His hand blesses the head of a *putto* as the genius of the arts, while its trophies are depicted at the foot of his dais,

---

[112] DeJean, 2005; Shawcross, 2014.

[113] Court portraits by William Larkin at Kenwood House also depict the female shoe. On the fenestration of Hardwick Hall 'more glass than wall' and the Hardwick embroideries, see Girouard, 1976.

Figure 24 Attrib. Nicholas Hilliard, Portrait of Elizabeth I in jewelled and embroidered dress and slippers, c. 1598, oil on canvas, Hardwick Hall Derbyshire (Photo: Wikimedia).

and through the arch onto the gardens of the Louvre the projected pyramid fountain. The blue mantle of French monarchy is decorated with gold-embroidered *fleur-de-lys* and lined with ermine surmounted by a lace ruff while his foot, prominently placed on a royally-decorated cushion, is shod in white silk with a pearl-laced organza bow cinched by a diamond buckle (**Fig. 25**). Thus, the notion of a glass-like textile slipper conceived as wholly beset with crystalline jewels and gemstones was not impossible.

In Straparola's Venice, and particularly at the lavish entertainments of carnival season, the decorated shoe was also on display along with every wealth of jewelled textile ornament. Like the fairy tale itself, this precious decorative footwear derived from Venetian trade to the East, especially Persia, then setting

Figure 25 Henri Testelin, *Louis XIV as patron of the arts*, 1668, oil on canvas, Château de Versailles (Photo: Réunion des Musées Nationaux).

fashion across the European courts. Perrault's glass slipper was surely in lightly parodic admiration of such court fashions. It was one that d'Aulnoy also described in her account of Princess Toutebelle's bridal dress as 'all of diamonds, down to her shoes', like a cascade of sunbeams.[114] Whether slippers, shoes, or mules, the jewelled toes and gilded ties of the epoch were set in juxtaposition to coloured-silk hose. Louis XIV's shoes were noted above all for their ornate heels, particularly the favoured *talons rouges*.[115] Decorated footwear was not new to the history of the French court – Charlemagne apparently bore shoes of occasion that were richly gilded and set with jewels as a manifestation of regal splendour, and sixteenth-century court portraits of

---

[114] D'Aulnoy, 2004, 550.
[115] Semmelhack, 2010, exemplified in Hyacinthe Rigaud's 1701 portrait of Louis XIV (Louvre).

Henri II and Catherine de Médicis manifest rose-fastened and embroidered shoes to complement their jewel-laden dress of luxury textiles (**Fig. 10**) – yet the baroque shoe defined at Versailles was acknowledged as an apogee. While few have survived due to the fragility of their materials, yet court portraits illustrate their critical place within a cultural imaginary of royal dress, as they are also represented in costume designs for the court ballet-balls that Louis XIV promoted and in which he performed himself.

As protection for the jewel-encrusted gilded or embroidered silk-textile court slipper, outer footwear conventionally comprised the mule, but also a range of wooden-platformed clogs, galoshes, chopines, or pattens, the latter term derived from hoof or *pattes*. These included decorated wooden stilt-shoes or metal-ring platforms, called 'pins', nailed into the base of the sole like a horseshoe, to offer further protection outdoors.[116] Particularly for women, the pins became an extension of the leg, adding height beneath the dress, and a sign of social distinction in their elevation, both literal and allegorical. In Basile's wryly comical rendition of Cenerentola, the besotted prince kisses such a shoe-pin that has captured his heart where once it imprisoned a lily-white foot, further comparing it to a candlestick, a tripod, a pedestal, through which 'she who sways my life was taller by a span and a half'.[117] For men, thick-soled leather galoshes or high-heeled boots ornamented variously with lace, silk taffeta, high-tops, gold buckles, and jewelled spurs were the mark of the cavalier, just as Perrault's *Puss-in-Boots* would acquire, as the sign of an assured social mastery at court. Like the Arabian fairy tale, the heeled riding-boot made for the stirrup came from the Middle East along with the Arab horse. At Louis XIV's address to his *Parlement* on 13 April 1655 in the name of his royal authority following the political ravages of the Fronde, the young king had appeared before them to forbid any further debate on his personal rule, attired in hunting dress and riding boots as the sign of his absolute monarchy sartorially configured in terms of equestrian command (**Fig. 26**).[118]

A freighted sign of legal possession in matters of land, estate, and marriage from antiquity, the emblematic status of the outer shoe would endure in language and image. Like the two pairs of Arnolfini pattens, one of wood and the other in decorative red (**Fig. 14**), their representation appears in myriad Dutch seventeenth-century genre paintings concerned with marriage and estate. A commonality of proverbs concerns the shoe as an idiom of social place – 'in your shoes', 'if the shoe fits'. They were also, proverbially, linked to the horse-patten or mule-shoe, as an outer protection to the hoof from archaic times.

---

[116] Semmelhack, 2010.   [117] Basile, 1891, I, 84; Basile, 1932, 60.
[118] Voltaire, 1966, I, 310. On Houasse, see Lett, 2020.

Figure 26 René-Antoine Houasse, *Equestrian portrait of Louis XIV in riding dress*, c. 1674, oil on canvas, Château de Versailles (Photo: Wikimedia).

The sign of the horse or mule-shoe was also laden with proverbial metaphors of possession and protection of estate: 'a shoe keeps a horse, a horse keeps a knight, a knight who can fight keeps his castle'. From such folklore arose the domestic practice of the horseshoe hung at entranceways as talismans of luck. Young women led astray were said to 'have lost a horseshoe', while a silver horseshoe was from antiquity fabled as a gift of good fortune at weddings, its curving horns lightly linked to the moon's crescent and so to a prospective fertility. This also lay behind early Renaissance arrangements of the hair into *cornettes*, as figured in the Arnolfini bride under her ruched white veil. A broadly conceived material metaphor of protection as of possession and desire, Ben Jonson writing of his mistress like Cinderella's prince 'would adore the shoe, and slipper was left off, and kiss it too . . . wrung on the withers by Lord Love'.[119] In Jean-Honoré Fragonard's depiction of Fortune's *Swing*, he

---

[119] Jonson, 1853, 'Let me be what I am', Elegy LX, 829–30.

Figure 27 Jean-Honoré Fragonard, *The Swing*, 1767, oil on canvas, Wallace Collection (Photo: Wikimedia).

painted a Cinderella-like satin mule-slipper cast into the air between two men, as the young woman rocks back and forth above them, her dress a billowing sail of pink silk (**Fig. 27**).[120]

4.2 Dress and Carriage

In Perrault's *Cinderella*, the fairy-godmother appears to the girl only at the point of her stepsisters' departure for the ball. As she is bidden by her fairy-guest, Cinderella fetches a pumpkin from the garden, along with mice and lizards, in a tale of enchanted manufacture. By magic, they are transformed into a golden carriage driven by six silver horses and a whiskered coachman, followed by

---

[120] Padiyar, 2020.

a further six footmen in livery, as befits a royal princess. With a final wave of her wand, the fairy-godmother transforms Cinderella's rags into a dress of gold- and silver-cloth gleaming with jewels, and a pair of glass slippers.[121] The prince is *enchanté,* while the other guests speak only of how to imitate her dress, if they can find such beautiful cloth and such able *couturiers.*

The fairy-tale accounts of her dress and carriage, in Perrault as in d'Aulnoy and Basile, are those of a bewitched manufacture. Here, the story touches not only on fairy-tale conventions of magical making but also on Renaissance cultures of alchemy, similarly rooted in classical antecedent and medieval legend. Alchemy comprised those methods of chemical enquiry seeking to transmute matter from one material to another. This concerned particularly the aspirational transmutation of base metals into gold, like fairy-tale transpositions of straw into riches. Much of alchemy's Renaissance knowledge was textual, concerned with the translation of treatises from the ancient languages as well as the anthological compilation of all types of alchemical lore, though in the hands of figures such as the sixteenth-century physician and alchemist Paracelsus it would also nurture experiment-based forms of scientific enquiry. A subject of kings, alchemy was sponsored across the European Renaissance courts, from Rudolf II's Prague and Tsar Michael I's Russia to Elizabeth I and Charles I, in the quest to discover the legendary medieval secrets attributed to Albertus Magnus on the transformation of stone into gold.[122] This led to the wide-ranging study of all chemical forms of matter, in order to discover those alchemical materialities apparently able to transform one substance into another.

Under the name of the philosopher's stone, as the appellation for all related forms of arcane alchemical knowledge, there was particular interest in those materials of a seemingly occult metamorphic manufacture, from the composition of precious metals to the quest for herbal elixirs purported to offer immortality. The 1612 publication of a hieroglyphics manuscript attributed to the Parisian manuscript-dealer of the early fifteenth century, Nicolas Flamel, was thought to suggest he had discovered the secret of their composition through his study of medieval lapidaries and herbaria. This claim was apparently furthered by publications such as the Dominican Donato d'Eremita's 1624 *Elixir of Eternal Life,* published in Naples and dedicated to Ferdinando II de' Medici. Purportedly based on the author's experimental research within a monastic pharmacy, the text is illustrated with diagrams of glass phials above furnaces in order to effect their magical-chemical transfusions.[123]

---

[121] Perrault, 1981, 173–4.   [122] From an extensive scholarship, Kren, 2013.
[123] Artephius [pseud.],1612; Donato d'Eremita, 1624.

Glass, like the pharmaceutical herbaria, silver, and above all gold, would be drawn into this constellation of apparently magical substances, at once material and immaterial, liquid and solid, forged in fire and as changeable as fate. Beyond the enchanted confection of Cinderella's glass slipper, her dress, like her carriage, was also an alchemical transfusion of the humble cinder-girl into royal gold.

Within a Renaissance history of dress and occasions of state, the social counterpart to Cinderella's magical transformation was that of royal dress, in the sartorial metamorphosis of women into queens. Descriptions of queenly attire was of costume so resplendent with gold and jewels as to rival the stars. At Catherine de Médicis' royal entry into Lyon in 1548, she appeared in a litter with the king's sister in gowns of rich gold- and silver-cloth studded with gems, while their headdresses were apparently so ornamented with resplendent stones that they seemed to rival the heavens. In Rouen, 2 October 1550, Queen Catherine was dressed in gold cloth embellished with gold embroidery, pearls, and precious stones, to resemble a sky sparkling with stars. At the christening of her daughter, Christine, in 1606, Queen Marie de Médicis was dressed in a gown said to be enriched with 32,000 pearls and 3,000 diamonds stitched into the cloth. For the 1697 wedding of Louis' grandson Louis, Duke of Burgundy, to Princess Marie-Adelaide of Savoy, at Versailles, the king's patronage of courtly *luxe* was of fairy-tale splendour, with guests in every colour of silk and velvet decorated with gold-thread embroidery garnished with gemstones, while the bride and groom were in cloth of spun-silver and gold encrusted with jewels, offset by a crown-diamond hairpiece and clusters of diamond buttons.[124] As a material and economic counterpart to a fairy-tale gown and carriage, the dress of queens was indeed fabled, seemingly of glittering jewels rather than cloth.

Such a wealth of precious materials for a queen's dress was predicated on the ever expanding Renaissance global trade in luxury commodities. The court ball-dress, and the sumptuous foods of Renaissance banqueting perquisite to such occasions, offer a microcosm of an early modern economic globalisation in material form. Gold and silver flowed from New World trade for currency as for jewellery, textile spangles, and thread; and from Africa, along with valuable ivory and ostrich feathers. Hauled by mule trains and then ships, their cargo became cultural emblems of the fortunes they carried. With these precious metals came valuable red cochineal dyes, chocolate, and fur. Amethysts came from Russia, as well as furs. Silks travelled thousands of miles of overland routes from China and India, along with tea, sugar, and valuable spices for

---

[124] Paresys, 2019; Arizzoli-Clémentel & Gorguet Ballesteros, 2009, 47–8.

perfume as for culinary production. Cargo from the East also carried pearls, diamonds, sapphires and rubies, camel-hair and cotton, as well as kermes red dyes, while the precious blue and purple mollusc dyes of Phoenician antiquity were from Turkey and Morocco, as was lapis lazuli, angora wool, and Persian pearls. Precious mineral dyes were used for colouring silks, enamels, china, and glass, in emulation of gemstones.

With the fall of Constantinople in 1453 Europe's travel through the East was severely circumscribed, so fuelling the quest for new routes via circumnavigation that led to the Cape of Good Hope, the Americas, and the Straits of Magellan, and the accelerating globalisation of an early modern mercantile economy. Within this expanding network of trade, glass beads and mirrors were as often currency as those of precious metals. In the words of the French merchant-adventurer Jean-Baptiste Tavernier, who would supply Indian diamonds to Louis XIV, traders carried 'little mirrors, enamelled rings, glass beads' as currency.[125] These were a staple of exchange for both the Canadian Hudson Bay Company, founded in 1670, and the Royal African Company of 1672, for the purposes of consolidated trading, proverbially known as the 'glass-bead companies'. Their use as currency is further manifest in Jacques Savary's *Dictionary of Global Commerce*, written for the use of merchant-traders such as himself, which offered a guide to exchange rates between artefacts such as glass beads, cowry shells, beaver pelts, and gold thread, as well as firearms and slave trafficking.[126] From the earliest voyage of Columbus, glass beads were the global mercantile exchange currency of the New World, traded for exotic potatoes, peppers, plantain, maize, fish, furs, and gold.

In Basile's *Cenerentola*, the prince's ball is composed of dancing and feasting over a succession of days in the manner of Renaissance festivities of marriage and occasion. Like his use of Neapolitan dialect, Basile's princely ballroom banquet is distinctively local; howsoever indebted to the fairy-tale banquets of the *Arabian Nights*, such gastronomic detail is also translated into the cultural idioms of Naples. Replacing Arabian sweetmeats and sherbets, there are *stufati*, *polpette*, *maccheroni*, and *ravioli*, and particularly the traditional Neapolitan Easter breads: *casatielli* made with pecorino and spiced-pork salami shaped in a wreath and decorated with eggs in their shells, and *pastiere* filled with sweetened ricotta further flavoured with lemon and orange blossom.[127] Equally, Cenerentola's fairy-benefactor is a fiction of food as wealth, for she is a tree spirit residing in a date palm of the south, whom the girl invokes by calling out '*dattolo d'oro*' to the abundant clusters of golden dates that are the

---

[125] Tavernier, 1676, I, 379.   [126] Savary, 1723; Trivellato, 2000, 241–3.
[127] Basile, 1891, I, 84.

fruit of this tree (as would also be the case in Grimm's *Aschenputtel* much later, though transfigured as a hazelnut tree).[128] Dates, oranges, and lemons were known across the Middle East from antiquity, and introduced to the southern Mediterranean by traders and returning Crusaders throughout the late Middle Ages; in Basile's Campania, they were a flourishing horticulture. His conclud- ing fairy tale of the *Pentamerone* was *The Three Citrons*, as another story of fairy-fated marriage orchestrated around a citrus tree and its gifts of fruit. For d'Aulnoy and Perrault, it is instead the princely offering of citrus fruit to Cinderella that emblematises the exquisite horticultural and culinary delicacies of Louis XIV's gastronomy. D'Aulnoy couples the royal gift of oranges from Portugal with sweets of *confitures* and *sucre* as French confections, howsoever the sugar of which they were made would have been imported from India or Brazil.[129]

While the bitter orange was long known across the medieval Mediterranean, sweet oranges were a luxury new to elite dining in fifteenth-century Europe, brought from the East, apparently by Vasco da Gama. With it came sugarcane, and so candied fruits and peel – *glacé*, like the *glace* of Louis' Hall of Mirrors in edible miniature. In Henri and Jean-Baptiste Bonnart's costume plates of the 1670s and 1680s, the orange-vendor calls: 'My oranges are from Portugal, their sweetness *regale*' in a verbal play of gifts and royalty.[130] As their depiction in the Arnolfini wedding portrait suggests, oranges were a precious commodity associated with the festive foods of occasion; both the fruit and the blossom were also valued ingredients in the facture of perfumes and pomanders (**Fig. 14**).

Louis XIV had a great love of the orange tree, building a monumental orangery for them at Versailles to protect them from winter frosts, and disposing them throughout the ceremonial rooms of the palace in solid-silver ewers. In their display, they were valued for their fragrant blossom as much as their golden citrus-scented fruit. When Louis XIV confiscated the estates of Nicolas Fouquet at neighbouring Vaux-le-Vicomte, this included over 1,000 orange trees then transferred to Versailles, as a measure of their perceived worth. Successor to the Louvre orangery of the early seventeenth century, and its earlier royal example at Château d'Amboise, Jules-Hardouin Mansart's Versailles orangery was Europe's largest, housing some 3,000 trees.

In Italy, the lemon would grow abundantly in the south and form a staple of its festive food and drink, while in the north, under Medicean husbandry, it flourished, particularly at Villa Medicea di Castello, where Niccolò Tribolo built the garden architecture. Here, the interests comprised decorative display of

---

[128] Basile, 1891, I, 83.   [129] Perrault, 1981, 174, 175; D'Aulnoy, 2004, 451.

[130] Henri & Jean-Baptiste Bonnart, *Recueil des modes de la cour de France*, 1670–93, https:// collections.lacma.org/node/205568 (last accessed 2021), plate 166.These were coloured prints for sale that might then be bound into volumes.

their scented blossom as well as horticulture of the fruit in the generation of specialised varieties through grafting, to produce chimera such as the mixed-colour green and gold *bizzarrie* as an *exemplum* of early modern scientific research in natural history. In Sicily and Spain, similar horticultural grafting promulgated the mixed-flesh blood oranges, or *sanguinello*.[131] This fruit was further known as *tarocco*, like the tarot or trump playing cards also imported from the Middle East to the Renaissance palace games-table. Sharing a Latin etymology of altercation or changeability, of colours as of cards, the *tarocco* cards were commonly conceived emblems of fortune, of prosperity, and reversals of fate. Comprising series of classical personifications as well as the statutory figures of a royal court, Renaissance playing cards were above all games of chance.[132] Similarly, the golden orange was the fruit of fortune. Long conflated with the 'golden apples' of mythology, as Straparola's tales also invoked, they were said to be the gift of the gods at the marriage of Zeus and Hera, and she delighted to grow them in her gardens at the Hesperides. Here, they might become gold itself, hence their enduring botanical denomination as *Hesperidoeidē*. The starred 'golden apple' of myth was also the mutable gift of the gods to the shepherd-prince Paris. Tasked to judge the beauties of Hera, Aphrodite, and Athena in return for Helen, his choice brought the onset of the Trojan War that would lead to the foundation of Rome, and the great transformations of destiny it wrought.

In Perrault's *Cinderella* the 'golden apple' also becomes, through a fairy-tale metamorphosis, both the *citrouille*-pumpkin of her kitchen garden and the gilded coach in which she will ride to the ball.[133] Also in d'Aulnoy's story of the ram with golden horns, the Princess Merveilleuse is invited to join the prince in a great pumpkin carriage fitted with velvet cushions in which they travel to a field of flowers, feasting, and fine liqueurs.[134] The details exemplify such fairy-tale narratives of inversion, from the folklore of the rustic vegetable patch as harvest pumpkins, to the royal carriages of princely estate. In a folkloric recollection of their vegetable use, manifest in the facture of all manner of vases and bottles from drinking carafes to luxury perfumes (**Figs. 2 and 4**), the gourd-shaped flask was the ubiquitous form of glass vessels, for water as for perfume. In Basile's account, Cenerentola's toilet comprises sprinkling her with cosmetic water from a rustic pumpkin flask, in a witty inversion of courtly gold, recalling also its folkloric dermatological-medicinal usages. Yet the harvest jack-o-lantern was also lightly haunted by legends of the *feu-follets* or will-o-the-wisps, conceived as the torchlit spirits of

---

[131] Freedberg, 1997.   [132] O'Bryan, 2019; Alligo, 2017.   [133] Perrault, 1981, 173.
[134] D'Aulnoy, 2004, 415.

abandoned and destitute women within popular rituals of Toussaint whose fairy-lights danced over the peatbogs where the pumpkin also readily grew. As such, the Cinderella story is shadowed by the spectre of its social inversion, of cinders and Cendron. Within the realm of the fairy tale, like the changeable fortune of an Apuleian Psyche, howsoever Cinderella is magically transported to the ball in a carriage of queens, at the stroke of midnight she will find herself abandoned once again to the wilderness of fickle fate.

The use of carriages by European royalty and aristocracy was an event of the sixteenth century, with significant consequences for urbanistic and architectural development in forging ever grander civic spaces for their transit. With the developing production of plate-glass for windows in the final decades of the seventeenth century, closed carriages were increasingly fashionable, in which the windows 'framed' the aristocratic occupants for display while also shielding them from direct contact. Their decoration was ever richer and more conspicuous, as the visible yet sealed sign of noble presence and passage throughout the city. Royal collections of coaches and carriages at Versailles, as elsewhere, manifest the wealth of their gold-leaf baroque sculptural decoration, lavish textile interiors of brocades and silk-velvets, gilded and painted wheels, and ornamental finials of mythological or heraldic design. The consortium of trades and materials required – wheel- and cartwrights, carpenters, metalsmiths, glass-window makers, sculptors and painters, gilders, seamstresses, tapestry-makers, and embroiderers – brought together artisanal artistry from what were often Crown appointments. At the marriage of Maria Anna of Austria – daughter of the Holy Roman Emperor, Leopold I – to the Portuguese King John V in 1708, the new queen travelled in procession through Lisbon in a carriage of gilded and carved wood decorated with crowned lions and her royal monogram upholstered in red velvet. Made in Austria in specific preparation for her nuptial entry, it was shipped to Lisbon in advance in order to carry her into the city in the manner of a royal bride (**Fig. 28**). Even leading court artists of the day such as Bernini played a part in carriage design, as for the coach that carried the newly converted Queen Christina of Sweden into Rome in 1655.[135] In the marriage of Grand-Duke Ferdinando de' Medici to Princess Christine de Lorraine in 1589, Christine's cortège through Tuscany and into Florence comprised gilded carriages in processional alternation with her appearance on a white horse covered in gold cloth, as d'Aulnoy emulated in her account of Cendron's Spanish mule.[136] Elsewhere, d'Aulnoy described enchanted carriages of mother-of-pearl drawn by hippogriffs, or miniature coaches made of gold and driven by

---

[135] Tyden Jordan, 1988.   [136] Saslow, 1996, 138–51.

Figure 28 Maria Anna of Austria 1708 wedding carriage, gilt wood, Museu Nacional dos Coches, Lisbon (Photo: Patrimonio Cultural, Portugal).

green mice for the carriage of marionettes. Such fairy-tale toys were, she adds, made by the celebrated Parisian puppeteers Brioché, who played at the fair of St Germain and at court for the Dauphin.[137] The wondrous gilded coaches of royal wedding processions produced a folkloric counterpart in Cinderella's fairy-tale harvest pumpkin, and in a host of traditional popular marriage games: the so-named *carrosse et cocher*, and the exchange of shoes or *chaussure mariage* of the bridal couple as a metaphor of shared destiny.

In Agostino Lampugnani's *Stagecoach, or Fashionable Dress* of 1648 the author set his light-hearted conversational text on the pitfalls and perils of fashion as of fortune within a travelling coach in which the passengers shared their reflections on clothing as a metaphor of moralities. A much-bowdlerised imitation of the dialogic literary form, the book is noted today chiefly for its title – *alla moda* – generally acknowledged as the first publication to use the phrase to signify fashion.[138] Lampugnani's literary stagecoach, an early form of public transport, carries a variety of people on their return from the fair at Bergamo, whose conversation composes his text. The seasonal fairs, as a mainstay of a medieval exchange economy that would continue across the seventeenth century and beyond, were long-established trading points of

---

[137] D'Aulnoy, 2004, 421, 246, 218. On the Brioché marionette theatre, Magnin, 1852, 135–42.
[138] Lampugnani, 1648; Paulicelli, 2014, 205–23.

a popular sociability and its attendant cultures of food, music, dancing, and travelling theatre. Thus, the social register was very different from the luxury merchandising of the rue St Honoré, or the royally-appointed *couturiers* of the court at Versailles. Lampugnani's text nonetheless illustrates a broad-based conception of *moda* in dress, and those who follow it, the *modanti*. Much of the humour is directed at perceived excesses of fashion, for men and women, notably of the impracticalities of the hoop-skirt and high-heeled pattens or pins. It also readily identifies the parts-dressing of the Renaissance wardrobe, in which collars, cuffs, ruffs, even sleeves were separate pieces that could be attached to different gowns or doublets, along with ribbons, rosettes, and other frippery, also illustrated in Elizabethan pattern-books or paper doll-clothes.

Within the comic diatribe of Lampugnani's characters, there is a common if shifting classification of dress, largely though not exclusively in terms of geographical difference: Spanish; French; Milanese; or Venetian. The humour is consequently driven by questions of cultural identity, which dress could both manifest and disguise. Centuries of sumptuary legislation had concerned the usurpation of social registers in matters of dress, while the sixteenth-century circulation of printed costume books represented clothing above all in terms of national or regional identities, like Lampugnani, as part of a larger geographical typology of cultural difference perceived as custom (*costume*), in dress, food, language, and dialect. In d'Aulnoy's *Cinderella*, the girl brings butter, milk, flour, and eggs to her godmother to make '*gâteau à la mode de notre pays*'. Pâtisserie, like clothing, is defined geographically, according to the custom or manner – *mode* – of its making. Elsewhere, however, d'Aulnoy details the court's fashion for chocolate, sugared almonds, muscat wines, champagne, *confitures*, and white-floured *pâtisserie* in terms of estate, in contrast to the black bread and cabbage of the *paysans,* or the rustic fare of her *bergers galants*, dining on eggs, butter, milk, hazelnuts, strawberries, and cherries. The lexical elision of making, in food as in other artefacts, is also carried into English, where fashion and 'to fashion', deriving from *facere* or *façon de faire*, are also synonyms for myriad artisanal manufactures. In step with a Renaissance history of textiles and clothing, this evolving lexicon would come to signify *la mode* or fashion above all as the synonym for dress. Thus, Renaissance *costume* was rendered in terms of an apparently timeless geography, while *la mode* in the age of Louis, howsoever we mark the transition, would come to be defined above all in terms of the temporal succession of styles.

In addition to paper-dolls and printed costume plates, national styles of Renaissance dress were also promulgated by means of miniature mannequins of clothing. With faces of porcelain, china, alabaster, painted papier-mâché, wood or embroidered silk, their clothes were made according to the same tailoring methods as for women, so that the clothing could be imitated in terms of material, pattern, and facture. Among Renaissance courts, these dolls carried the styles of other realms between them. Thus, Federico Gonzaga, present at the French court in 1515, wrote on behalf of François I to his mother, Isabella d'Este, for a doll so that women of the court in Paris might dress in the Italian fashion, for, as in all aspects of culture, this French Renaissance king was intent on procuring Italy's leading reputation on behalf of France. Federico asked that the doll have a full complement of clothing: 'the king wishes My Lady to send him a doll dressed in the style that you wear, as to the jacket, sleeves, under- and outer-garments, dresses and headdress, and the dressing of your hair'. Isabella readily acceded, also sending such a doll to the Spanish court at the request of her son Ferrante in 1524 on behalf of Eleanora of Austria, sister to Charles V, for the purpose of fashioning dresses for her ladies-in-waiting.[139] These royal costume-dolls were international gifts of finely-detailed craft, made for princesses in the luxury fabrics of court dress (**Fig. 29**). D'Aulnoy's Prince Lutin recounts the story of a princess desirous to know the fashions of other courts, whose prince therefore seeks out fabrics on his travels to China and Siam, then made into doll-clothes by Parisian seamstresses for her.[140]

Clothed mannequins were also produced as part of the elaborate preparations for royal weddings, in which detailed information as to textile patterns and design might be exchanged between the courts involved. This was particularly important in crafting the new queen's sartorial identity, as a carefully negotiated element of courtly cultural exchange in which the princess of one country, along with her maids of honour, was transfigured into the idiom of another. At Christine of Lorraine's 1589 Florentine entry to become Ferdinando de' Medici's bride, her passage from French princess to Tuscan Grand-Duchess was marked in dresses prepared for her in advance by the grand-ducal wardrobe. Appearing first in a gown of gold cloth styled in the French manner, after the ceremonies she was instead dressed in white in a Florentine cut to attend the lavish banquets and entertainments in honour of their marriage.[141] When the Spanish royal Infanta Maria Teresa became Louis XIV's queen of France, her royal progress was similarly marked by a symbolic modification of her dress as she travelled, leaving behind her Spanish *guardainfante* to don the French *fleur-de-lys*, along with her great retinue of ladies-in-waiting. This was an event long in the preparation and much dedicated to matters of royal custom, like

---

[139] Pearce, 2018, 7.   [140] D'Aulnoy, 2004, 249–50.   [141] Saslow, 1996, 138–51.

Figure 29 Daniël van den Queborn, *Portrait of Louise Juliana of Orange-Nassau*, c. 1582, Siegerlandmuseum, Siegen (Photo: Siegerlandmuseum).

those for Marie de Médicis to Henri IV.[142] On 24 July 1600, Henri IV sent mannequin-dolls and a French tailor to his prospective Tuscan bride Marie to instruct her and her ladies-in-waiting in the French manner of dress.[143] The bridalwear of queens was vested with the timeless symbols of national costume, at the same time representing the new queen as the apogee of the latest court fashions.

Princely inventories indicate the extent of these court costume-dolls, as royal portraits of children also do (**Fig. 29**). Precious examples include a figure at the Royal Palace of Stockholm apparently belonging to Princess Katarina, daughter of Karl IX, from around 1600, in a gown of purple silk with gold lace, further decorated with red-silk sleeves and a muff ornamented with gold-thread embroidery and pearls. The mannequin further illustrates courtly hair-styling,

---

[142] Albero, 2016.   [143] Pearce, 2018, 9

with real hair-clippings fashioned into an intricate arrangement of braids studded with pearls and a gold-thread diadem.[144] Such courtly ambassadorial dress-
dolls became known among the '*précieuses*' in Parisian *salons* of Louis' reign
as Pandora-dolls, so-named in ludic recognition of changeable French fashion, à
la mode. Like a metaphorical Pandora's box or cornucopia of French commerce
and culture, the *Pandore* marked the growing shift from timeless costume to
timely fashion. Scant remaining testimony suggests these jointed wooden
figures were also made by marionette-makers, as, for example, the Parisian
sieur de Vandiet, 'sculptor of marionettes and mannequins' according to the
1692 edition of *L'Annuaire de Paris*.[145] D'Aulnoy's Sleeping-Beauty-like story
of 'Le serpentin vert' is particularly rich in details of Parisian fashion and dress;
the princess is attended by miniature china-dolls called '*pagodes*' in lexical
imitation of the '*pandores*', who stage mock battle with the evil queen's
marionettes led by a general Polichinelle. Combining the realms of costume-
dolls and child's play within the *salon* fairy tale, d'Aulnoy's story touches on the
material fabrication of the mannequin as a wooden marionette with a china-doll
face, as well as the developing fashion for *chinoiserie* that would shortly sweep
through all aspects of Parisian *luxe*.[146]

The extent of early fashion's elaboration through the mannequin-doll is also
manifest in a bridal couple known as Lord and Lady Clapham, of the 1690s,
with a remarkable complement of detachable clothes of manufactured fashion.
Their clothing includes shoes of silver silk-brocade tied with a pink ribbon,
knitted silk stockings, petticoats, overcoats, and mantua gowns, a mask for
fancy-dress balls, as well as jewellery comprising diamond-glass earrings and
a gold wedding band, suggesting a complete *trousseau* or household inventory
of their dress in miniature (**Figs. 30a** and 30b).[147] Cabinets of such costume-
dolls are also found in royal inventories of Catherine de Médicis, Henry VIII,
and Elizabeth I, with figurines dressed in velvet, satin, silver cloth, and gold
jewels, testament to their princely status as collectibles of luxury facture and
representations of court dress design. An Edinburgh Castle inventory of 1578
included costume-dolls seemingly as models for the ladies-in-waiting at Mary
Queen of Scots' court, transported by a miniature litter 'lynnit with crammosie
satine and steikit with harnessing thairto and tua little chyres in it and a cordoun

---

[144] Pandore, 1590s, Livrustkammaren Museum, the Royal Palace, Stockholm, court costume
collection; Dahlberg, 1996.
[145] Spadaccini-Day, 2009.
[146] D'Aulnoy, 2004, 583. *A la pagode* was also used for fashion inspired by trade with China
through Colbert's institution of the French global trade companies, as, for example, for men's
sleeves circa 1697, Marly, 1987, 89.
[147] https://collections.vam.ac.uk/search/?q=%20lady%20clapham&page=1&page_size=15 (last
accessed 2021).

(a)   (b)

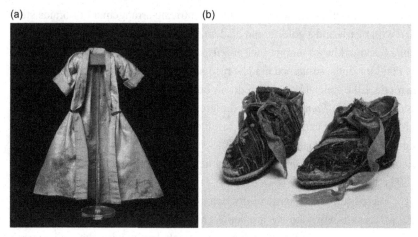

Figure 30a and Figure 30b Lady Clapham silk doll-clothes and embroidered
slippers, 1690-1700, Victoria & Albert Museum
(Photo: Victoria & Albert Museum)

of silk and gold'. In the sixteenth-century inventories of the Château d'Etelan
was the Petit Cabinet of Mademoiselle de Brissac, so-named for its miniature-
doll artefacts, which also comprised a toy litter as the carriage of queens. Built
for two passengers, the dolls' litter was of cramoisy velvet garnished with gold
passements, driven by two mules and accompanied by two pages, followed by
two further figures riding white horses.[148] Within a Renaissance imaginary of
collections as objects of curiosity and wonder, such cabinets of miniatures
might comprise costume-dolls and their household goods, as also invoked in
literary collections of fairy tales in the manner of d'Aulnoy's '*Collection-
Cabinet of Tales*'.

Reflecting the shifting place of luxury within Colbert's mercantilist economic
policies, Henri and Jean-Baptiste Bonnart's late seventeenth-century coloured
fashion-plates, titled *Collection of Fashion at the French Court*, followed the
new nomenclature of *moda* that Lampugnani's text suggested. Marking the
transition of noble dress from national costume to timely fashion, its fulsome
range of illustrated plates included both. In effect, costume dress became fancy
dress, as was the social practice of court for Louis' lavish masquerades. Indian,
African, and Arabian costumes appear alongside those of the *commedia del-
l'arte* characters, Arlequin, Polichinelle, and Scaramouche. Costume dress of
gallant rustics and shepherds were also worn at Louis' court balls, along with
masks of the crown trades of architects, painters, sculptors, and musicians who

---

[148] Pearce, 2018.

Figure 31 Henri & Jean-Baptiste Bonnart, Dame en habit de ballet, *Recueil des modes de la cour de France*, 1670-93, Los Angeles County Museum of Art (Photo: LACMA).

fabricated such entertainments.[149] Among them is a *Lady in a Ballgown,* in a richly-brocaded and embroidered dress with matching textile slippers, further ornamented with an exuberance of rosettes, ribbons, jewels, a swirling veil, and crowned by a feathered headdress in imitation of court fashion (**Fig. 31**). In Bonnart's plates, these appear as part of the accoutrement of the Parisian *mondaines* for ballroom wear. Bonnart's *modanti* of the rue St Honoré are

---

[149] Bonnart, 1670–93, https://collections.lacma.org/node/205568 (last accessed 2021), plates 132–7, comprising fancy-dress costumes of architects, painters, sculptors, musicians, as well as a shoemaker; Cugy, 2017; Marly, 1987, 61–79, 103–21.

otherwise dressed for promenade in the Tuileries gardens or boudoir receptions in the palaces of the Marais and the Faubourg St Germain. One of many such examples, Bonnart's fashion-plates formed part of what historians have described as a new 'fashion-press' of the late seventeenth century, inaugurated by Colbert in his concerted reordering of a national French economy. 'Fashion is to France what the gold mines of Peru are to Spain', Colbert is reputed to have said, by which he meant the manufacture and marketing of French luxury in the form of textiles for dress as well as furnishings and interior decoration that Louis' reign would so successfully promote.[150] Following the traditional calendar of the seasonal fairs, Colbert initiated the promotion of new textiles and patterns through an annual fashion-cycle of *Winter* and *Summer* collections, variously accompanied by muffs or parasols. The Parisian merchant-haberdasher Jacques Savary's 1675 manual on commercial trade, *The Perfect Shop-Keeper,* humorously allegorised the constantly shifting nature of French fashion as an aspect of national character, as changeable as the fortunes it carried.[151]

The monthly court review, *Le Mercure Galant*, launched by Jean Donneau de Visé in 1672, carried news of Versailles, including its newly seasonal fashions, to a wide readership across France and beyond, extending from London to St Petersburg. Its readers then emulated the designs in buying French goods as Colbert intended.[152] Alongside this nascent fashion magazine, the Renaissance costume-dolls of royal national dress were now reconceived as large-scale mannequins, dressed in the latest *couturier* styles from Paris and sent to all the courts of Europe to promote French luxury. At court, Louis XIV deployed his courtiers as ambassadors of French fashion within Colbert's patriotic orchestration of the national manufactories, advancing fashion as a vital element of the French political economy. At Louis' accession, as Colbert shrewdly recognised, court luxuries were perceived in terms of imports: Flemish tapestries, Venetian mirrors, Italian lace, and cloth were the materials of French royal and aristocratic *moeurs*. Colbert reversed this flow of trade with the establishment of the French Royal manufactories, inculcating and even imposing national loyalty in the acquisition of *luxe*. In the vast expansion of highly skilled French artisanal labour to serve expanding markets for its fashions, new legislation of the 1670s further recognised the economic position of working women as the *maîtresses, couturières*, and *marchandes de mode*, in addition to the traditional tailors' guilds, to serve the *haut monde* of the rue St Honoré and the female court at Versailles. Among the most renowned *couturières* in the pages

---

[150] Ubiquitously cited, if likely apocryphal, Fouchard, 2005, 31.
[151] Savary, 1675, I, 305; Jones, 2004 on the perceived 'inconstancy' of French fashion.
[152] Vincent, 2005.

of the *Mercure Galant* were Mesdames du Creux, Villeneuve, Rémond, Prévot, and Charpentier as the forerunners of Marie Antoinette's Rose Bertin. As markets for female clothing began to double those for men, so did the numbers of seamstresses who worked in women's fashions, increasingly independent of the male tailor. '*La mode* is the mirror of history', Louis supposedly said.[153] Cinderella's fairy-godmother of magical manufactures had a social match.

4.3 The Looking Glass

As Cinderella's stepsisters prepare for the ball, in Perrault's account they preen themselves before a mirror with her assistance. The mirror is full-length, Perrault specifies, allowing the stepsisters – and Cinderella – a view of their clothing as well as the grooming of their hair, and the stepsisters are, as Perrault relates, always before it.[154] Thus, the mirror is a vanity, in that it captures within its reflective surface the puffed-up airs of the stepsisters alongside the veiled beauty of the cinder-girl dressed in rags. The looking glass was a narrative emblem Perrault had used before, in his 1661 satire of social metamorphosis, *The Mirror of Orante*. A 'mirror-image' portraitist, Orante (his name a parody of the courtier's fawning awe or *orans*) is transformed into a mirror himself, so twining together the artist with his object-oeuvre in a literary fusion of people and things.[155] In Perrault's Cinderella, the looking glass becomes the site of a gentle social parody of the female toilet, before which the stepsisters plan their appearance at the royal ball:

> [they] could talk of nothing but what they were going to wear. The elder one said: 'I shall put on my red velvet dress and my English lace.' The younger one said: 'I shall put on the skirt I always wear, but to compensate, I shall have my cape with golden flowers and my diamond hairpin . . . .' They sent for the best hairdresser to style their hair into two rows of *cornettes,* as well as black taffeta beauty marks.[156]

The details of costume are also lightly comic in the mix of old and new, particularly in the description of the hair dressing in *cornettes* – a late medieval fashion revived in the 1670s with the addition of lace headscarves. English lace was, of course, banned at Versailles, along with Italian and Flemish wares, in the so-called 'lace wars' that Colbert waged throughout the 1660s, in which French manufacture would be ascendant, thereby casting the stepsisters as bearers of both out-of-date and contraband fashions.[157] This was something Perrault

---

[153] Ubiquitously, if likely apocryphally, attributed to Louis XIV, cited in Ribeiro, 1995, 3.
[154] Perrault, 1981, 171.   [155] Perrault, 1661.
[156] Perrault, 1981, 172, see also notes 10–14; Perrault, 2009, 131.
[157] Marly, 1987, 48; Kraatz, 1989, 45-50.

would touch on directly in his *Sleeping Beauty*, albeit in a gentle courtly *ludens*, for the princess who has just awoken from her century-long slumber is apparently dressed like a grandmother, with a high starched collar (**Figs. 10** and **29**), though he kindly notes she is radiantly beautiful the same.[158] In Basile's version of the story, the mirror is instead among the gifts of the fairy to Cenerentola, accompanied by a bevy of fairy-bridesmaids to dress her so that she too may go to the ball. Like Straparola, her preparatory toilet is marked in artefacts of luxury glass, albeit comically rendered in the rustic form of the pumpkin flask:

> A band of maidens came out, one with a mirror and one with a pumpkin flask, one with curling tongs and another with rouge, one with a comb and another with hairpins, one with dresses and one with necklace pendants and earrings. They all placed themselves around her and made her as beautiful as a sun and then mounted her in a coach with six horses accompanied by footmen and pages in livery.[159]

In a bejewelled version, La Force's fairy-tale toilet in her 'Plus belle que fée' (the title a pun of beauty's fairy-fate) describes a precious room of marvels decorated with great crystal mirrors with orangery-scented blossom set in gold vases garnished with rubies, and gemstone ewers of flowers, in which the princesses are bathed in magically-medicinal *eau de vie* and then sent on a dangerous quest for the cosmetically magical blush of youth, as the bewitched ingredients of an everlasting beauty.[160] Orange blossom was among the most highly valued of scents at Versailles, as well as at the court of Naples, where Basile served. Here the accounts are folkloric and fairy-tale variations of a bridal toilet, transforming girls into an apparently immortal and demiurge beauty as radiant as the sun, just as Louis' royal *levée* would also be configured into a cosmic apogee at the court of the sun-king.

Among the plethora of coloured plates for Bonnart's *Fashions of the French Court*, a number depict 'Ladies at their toilet' as a site of luxury cosmetic display. While the majority of the illustrations depict fashionable men and women in scenes of sociability, those of the toilet represent its preparations, albeit wrapped within cultural conventions of emulation, on the one hand of the court *levée* or the bridal toilet, and on the other of Venetian Renaissance painted mythological representations of the Toilet of Venus. Here, the pictorial genre of Venus at her toilet inaugurated by Giovanni Bellini, Titian, Veronese, and Tintoretto, is transformed into a gentle comedy of manners on the commerce of French fashion (**Figs. 32** and **5**). Among Bonnart's plates is a woman dressed in elaborately laced petticoats sitting at her dressing table, where the

---

[158] Perrault, 1981, 136.   [159] Basile, 1891, I, 83; translation adapted from Basile, 1932, 59.
[160] La Force, 1697, VI, 1–35.

Femme de qualité estant a sa toilette

Figure 32 Henri & Jean-Baptiste Bonnart, Femme de qualité estant a sa toilette, *Recueil des modes de la cour de France*, 1670–93, Los Angeles County Museum of Art (Photo: LACMA).

conventional accoutrements of her grooming are arranged before her: a double-sided ivory comb, a gilt-casket for jewels, a draped-silk *peignoir* to the side, and two mirrors in ornamental frames with gilt-*ormolu* mounts, comprising a large wall-mounted looking glass and a smaller matching mirror used to view the back of the head in preparing the intricate coiffures of the period. Her pose is nonchalant, her body elegantly crossed above the gilt-upholstered boudoir stool on which she sits. Her abundantly draped skirts move across her leg to reveal a glimpse of red lining beneath, matched by her mule-slipper, seemingly of gold-embroidered cloth surmounted by a red-silk frill.

While Bonnart's plates of the *haute* trades in seeming fancy dress comprise architects, painters, sculptors, and musicians in a light-hearted parody of their 'part' in the orchestration of aristocratic sociability, other engravings such as Nicolas de Larmessin's late seventeenth-century '*Costumes of the Mechanicals*' included a range of the crown trades of courtly service: silversmiths, jewellers, tailors and dressmakers, hatmakers, playing-card makers, as well as parfumiers, glass-makers and mirror-makers in the service of majesty, many of great wealth and renown. Here, the figure of the mirror-maker appears fully dressed in mirrors, like a ballroom chandelier himself, wittily looking through his dainty telescope in a playful social guessing-game of 'who-views-who' (**Fig. 33**).[161] Similarly, the figure of the glass-window maker wears the tools of his trade in fancy dress, comprising heeled court shoes with bows made of crossed glass-cutters. Larmessin's prints are eloquent in drawing together the range of luxury glassware promulgated at the court of Louis XIV, from the decorative to the scientific. The mirror-maker print brings together the dressing-table and the ballroom but also the optical instruments and technologies that drove the new sciences of lens-based observation in the age of Galileo. Above all, it represents the burgeoning commerce of the French royal manufactories, of which glass was among the first.

At court, jewelled dressing-table mirrors were royal gifts of renown. Variously made of rock-crystal or *cristallo* glass and foiled with silver as the most radiant of metals, such mirrors were kept among the crown jewels as rare court possessions of the highest rank. In the extensive inventories of Louis' jewellery, as of his royal '*présents*' to princesses, duchesses, and queens, silver-gilt toiletry mirrors were valued as regal gifts of the first order.[162] These mirror frames were highly-wrought decorative surfaces of precious metals and gems often of mythological or allegorical composition and jewelled metaphors of their courtly reigns (**Fig. 34**).[163]

Within a jeweller's and goldsmith idiom of Renaissance court luxury, the sparkling reflection of glass or crystal mirrors was conceived not only to enhance light, but as an artefactual metaphor of light itself. Galland's translation of the *Arabian Nights*, equally, shone with jewelled light, as also the fairy tales of the *salons*. Such shimmering immateriality was embodied in the jinni, the Arabian object-fairies who executed their masterful magic on behalf of their owners. Jinni or genies, as they were translated within early modern literary cultures of ingenuity, sprang magically from burnished lamps, gleaming bottles, and glittering glass caskets, as the lustrous object-repositories of good fortune in which they were housed. Like object-metaphors of the nested

---

[161] Pullins, 2014.   [162] Thépaut-Cabasset & Warner, 2007–8.   [163] Alcouffe, 2001, 391–3.

Figure 33 Nicolas de Larmessin, Miroitier-Lunettier, *Arts et métiers*, c. 1695, British Museum (Photo: British Museum).

Arabian fairy tale itself, these lightsome containers were configured as allegorical artefacts of destiny. Throughout, the tales are suffused with the emblematic elision of diamond, crystal, and glass, as the materialities of light's reflections, and the underlying magic of Scheherazade's stories in bringing light relief to the shadows of the Sultan's mind. Paradigmatically, Aladdin's cave glitters with gold, silver, and gemstones of such size and iridescence he mistakes them for glass. In the story of the poor rope-maker

Figure 34 Crystal mirror with jewel and gold frame (agate, sardonyx, garnet, diamond, enamel, emerald, cameo), c. 1630–5, (formerly known as the Marie de Médicis mirror), Musée du Louvre (Photo: Réunion des Musées Nationaux).

Hassan Alhabbal, the wheel of fortune turns on a fish with a diamond in its belly so large as to light his home like a magic lamp, and thereafter his life, in making him a wealthy merchant of renown.[164] The gleaming gold and jewels that bespangle these stories are, throughout, metaphors of light itself, further configured in terms of glass objects as the foremost manufactured materiality of solar reflection. At Versailles too, this cosmic perception of light-reflective materials comprised the scintillation of gemstones, particularly crystal, long understood as precious allegories of light and so of the *Roi Soleil*. In its aspirations to luxury, gemstone light-reflection was what Renaissance glass manufacture strove to emulate. In this regard, the cultural perception of glass was not only of a wondrous metamorphic material, but also a marvellously

---

[164] Galland, 1704–17. 'Aladdin ou la lampe merveilleuse', split between volumes 9–10, 37–8; 'Histoire de Cogia Hassan Alhabbal', also split between volumes 10–11, 42–3.

mimetic one. In the words of the fifteenth-century Venetian scholar Marcantonio Sabellico, 'there is no type of precious stone in existence that has not been imitated by the glass industry; a sweet contest between nature and man'.[165] Within a cultural imaginary of glass as a material with a gem-like *cristallo* sparkle, both Louis' glass mirrors and Cinderella's glass slipper were prismatic representations of royal *éclat*.

The history of glass production underpinning the luxury mirror that Colbert sought in the establishment of its manufacture in France depended on an industrialised chemistry of materials, between artisanal practice and scientific enquiry. As Perrault allegorised in his *Cabinet of the Arts* of 1690, the accomplishments of the French Academy depended on the artisanal *arts et métiers*, comprising the practice of optics and the mechanics of craft alongside its theoretical elaboration. For the mirror, like the glass lens, was not only an instrument of Galilean science but also the product of it. This is already manifest in sixteenth-century publications of natural history such as the Neapolitan Giambattista della Porta's widely published 1589 *Natural Magic*, concerning the chemistry of glass as well as its optical applications, or Leonardo Fioravanti's *Speculum of Science*, published in Venice in 1564, on the lens-based instruments of science and medicine as the critical tools of its practice.

Like *cristallo* glass itself, much of the artisanal literature on glassmaking came from Venice, as in Antonio Neri's *Art of Glass-Making* of 1612, the first published collection of Venetian recipes for glass, which Jean Haudicquier De Blancourt then adapted for the French court in 1697. Both drew on Vannoccio Biringuccio's consideration of mirror-making within his *Pirotechnics* published in Venice in 1540, as an aspect of Renaissance chemistry in its concern with materials forged in fire such as metalwork and glass.[166] Courtly interest in the metamorphic 'art' of glass is also manifest in the painted decorations for Francesco de' Medici's *studiolo* in Palazzo Vecchio, executed under the jurisdiction of Giorgio Vasari in the 1570s, where the scenes included a representation of the prince visiting a glassmaking furnace in the name of Prometheus, as the sign of scientific research in chemistry and alchemy alike.[167]

The much-emulated and allegorised play of material resemblance between glass and gems rested on a long textual tradition of medieval lapidaries dedicated to the nature and uses of minerals, which remained in continuous consultation across the sixteenth and seventeenth centuries alongside newly emerging treatises on early modern geology and chemistry. Texts such as Thomas Nichols' *A Lapidary or the History of Pretious Stones* of 1652 and Anselm de

---

[165] Sabellicus, 1560, III, 1, 'De Venetae Urbis situ'.
[166] Porta, 1589; Neri, 1612; Fioravanti, 1564; Biringuccio, 1540; Haudicquier, 1697.
[167] Conticelli, 2007.

Boodt, physician to Rudolf II's *History of Gemstones*, published in Hanover in 1609, continued to evaluate minerals for their perceived apotropaic properties in the manner of the medieval medical lapidaries. Yet, the seventeenth century also produced texts dedicated to the stratigraphic geology of crystals such as the Danish Niels Stensen or Nicolaus Steno. Dedicated to the Medici, Steno's 1669 treatise analysed the internal crystal-facet structure itself, under the lens of the newly developed microscope.[168] Thus, the seventeenth-century conception of 'crystal' spanned scientific and decorative uses, comprising chemistry and optics, gemstones and glass.

Within medieval lapidaries, as in the goldsmiths' fabrication of jewellery, rock-crystal was among the most precious of gems. Valued for its powers of magnification and transparency as the so-named *lapis specularis* or spectacle stone, it was celebrated above all for its prismatic reflection of light. Medieval Celtic crystals such as the Clach-na-bratach were regarded as prophetic on account of their shifting constellations of refracted illumination. This is further manifest in folkloric descriptions of flint's glassy 'seeing stones' or 'druids' eggs' such as the Scottish legend of Kenneth Mackenzie or the Germanic *Hühnergötter*, as also the volcanic obsidian-glass of Elizabeth I's magus, Dr John Dee.[169] If scientific analysis of light's refractive spectrum awaited the studies of Isaac Newton, medieval lore and legend had long heralded crystal's brilliant sparkle or 'fire'. Crystal was privileged over all other gemstones within medieval cultures, while the diamond's ascendance awaited the seventeenth century, hence the earlier approximation of glass manufacture to crystal in a material imaginary of crystalline. Prior to the sixteenth century, gemstones were simply polished into a dome and set in a rounded or cabochon shape; such settings privileged size, in which diamonds were generally the smallest stones, particularly compared to crystal.

 Until the greatly accelerating early modern precision-skill in cutting gemstones, driven as much by demand for optical glass-lenses for spectacles and scientific instruments as by jewellers, diamond was only one of many precious stones and chiefly valued for its industrial use in cutting adamantine materials, among them gems and glass. This is manifest not only in the realm of jewellery and lenses but also in the prismatic crystal-glass cuts for chandeliers as would ornament the Hall of Mirrors at Versailles. Over the course of the sixteenth century, in tandem with growing scientific accuracy in the fabrication of optical lenses, gem-cutters such as the Flemish Lodewyk van Berken, the Genoese

---

[168] Nichols, 1652; Boodt,1609, Stensen, 1669.

[169] www.donnachaidh.com/stories-clach_na_bratach.html (last accessed 2021); www.britishmuseum.org/collection/object/H_1966-1001-1 (last accessed 2021); Hahn & Shalem, 2020.

Giacomo Tagliacarne, and the Tuscan Giovanni delle Corniole developed incised gemstone-cuts of ever finer complexity and detail. Emeralds, sapphires, and amethysts, in particular, were increasingly presented as squared-off with bevelled edges in what was known as a mirror-cut, in emulation of the flashing lustre of a mirror reflection. Such crown jewels of state as Elizabeth I's gifted 'Mirror of Portugal', 'Mirror of France', and 'Mirror of Great Britain', the latter made in commemoration of the union of the crowns in 1603, were cut to display their size and to signify their light-filled perspicacity as a metaphor of enlightened rule. Smaller diamond crystals might also be presented as crystal points or 'sparkes'.

It was only with the more elaborate prismatic cuts developed circa 1600 that diamonds came to the fore, precisely for their adamantine ability to sustain far greater tooling and so a growing multiplicity of chiselled facets, and above all for their *cristallo* transparency that could display a full range of internal light refraction as 'sparkle'.[170] Cardinal Giulio Raimondo Mazarin's fêted collection of diamonds, which he later bequeathed to the French Crown, were displayed by his chosen court jewellers in multi-faceted rose-cuts to highlight their scintillating light, while Louis XIV's own interest in crystalline gems and, especially, diamonds led him to acquire, among others, the starred '*Bleu de France*' or Blue (now Hope) Diamond from the much-travelled merchant-prince of gems, Tavernier (**Figs. 35** and **36**).[171] While the ascendance of the diamond depended on the increased artisanal knowledge of gem-cutters, the seventeenth-century recognition of light's refraction into a prismatic spectrum was Newton's, itself dependent on the skill of glass-cutting for lens-based instruments of vision that led early modern scientific enquiry in the age of Galileo. Thus, the scientific study of light, as of the stars, was founded in lens- and mirror-based instruments fabricated from glass, cut with the equivalent tools and precision skills for telescopes as for gems.

Within the further apartments of Louis XIV's rooms beyond the Hall of Mirrors were housed the king's collections-cabinets, comprising books and pictures but above all the objects of precious reflective materials he prized – lustrous gold- and silver-filigree, sparkling gemstones, and light-filled rainbow-prisms of rock-crystal.[172] D'Aulnoy's *Golden Branch* described in fairy-tale form these royal cabinets and collections, for the prince *Sans-Pair* (surely an allegory of Louis as without paragon) has libraries of illuminated vellum manuscripts, galleries of portraits, and a prized cabinet of glittering rock-crystal, amber, and mother-of-pearl that opened with an emerald key.[173] Louis

---

[170] Strong, 1966; Bycroft & Dupré, 2019.　　[171] Tavernier, 1676.　　[172] Saule, 2010.
[173] D'Aulnoy, 2004, 303–6.

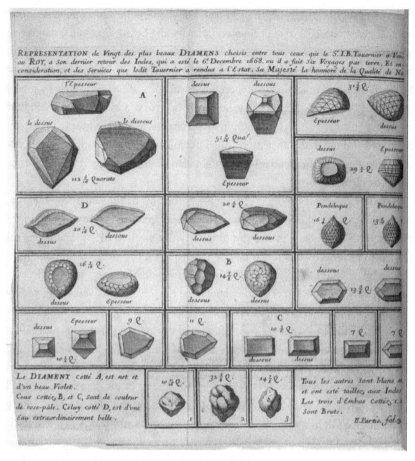

Figure 35 Jean-Baptiste Tavernier, *Les six voyages*, II, *Indes*, Paris 1676,
plate of diamonds acquired in India illustrating what would come
to be regarded as 'le bleu de France' (A), and a succession of diamond cuts
including prismatic rose cuts (B) and mirror cuts (C). (Photo: Gallica).

XIV's cabinet-collections of crystalline artefacts, like Perrault's imaginary
glass slipper, arose at the centre of a cosmic conceptualisation of reflected
light as metaphors of royalty, lodged within crystals, diamonds, glass, and the
resplendent mirrors of Versailles' great gallery. On the walls of his cabinets,
further mirrors enhanced the display. Executed to the designs of the king's court
artist and director of the Gobelins, Charles Le Brun, under the auspices of the
royal gold- and silversmith Girard Debonnaire in 1677, they were over 3 metres
in height and weighed 500 kilograms each, framed in solid silver with decorative trophies and festoons of flowers and fruit surmounted by the arms of

Figure 36 Hope Diamond (Le bleu de France), Smithsonian Institute
(Photo: Smithsonian Institute).

France.[174] Such mirrors not only lent light to the cabinet, they enabled viewing objects in-the-round. As *Wunderkammern* cabinets of wonder, Louis' crystals were related to broader court patronage of optical science manifest throughout the king's collections, in France as elsewhere. For crystal-prisms, glass-lenses, and mirrors were kept side by side, as related materials and artefacts of magnified vision and the conduct of light.

These were precisely the years when Newton developed and demonstrated to the Royal Society in London his theory of prismatic light refraction in water droplets, informed by the study of mirrors as the scientific demonstration of light's passage. In Paris, Louis' Academy appointment, the brilliant Dutch scientist and astronomer Christiaan Huygens, would go on to publish his *Treatise on Light* of 1690 in dialogue with Newton, regarded as the first

---

[174] Arminjon, 2007, 46, 77, 235, illus. no. 13.

mathematical theorisation of light rays based on the observation of catoptric reflection. It was testimony to the fecund cultures of seventeenth-century research centred on mirrors, optics, and light that nurtured scientific and artisanal developments side by side.[175] The nature of this research advanced a rich interplay between catoptrics, as the study of the visual effects of reflection through glass mirrors, with dioptrics, or the science of light's passage instanced in the analytical calculation of its refractions witnessed in gemstones. At the same time, an ever accelerating practice-based interest in developing glass-lenses for microscopes and telescopes grew up alongside Colbert's institution-alisation of French glass-manufacturing.[176] As was characteristic of baroque princely patronage, Louis' collecting interests also comprised telescopic instru-ments of science, wrought in regal silver and gold casements. Astronomy, in particular, was considered the 'science of kings', through its solar and cosmic associations with astrology. Its instruments – astrolabes, quadrants, and, above all, telescopes made up of different types of glass-lenses and mirrors – became royal collectibles assembled in the collectors' cabinets of the European courts, as well as in France.[177] Along with the establishment of the Academy of Sciences in 1666, Louis and Colbert also established the French Royal Observatory the following year. Attracting Europe's chief astronomers, it became the leading centre for astronomical research of the late seventeenth century. Among them was Huygens, who first identified Saturn's ring and moons, and whose research was subsequently furthered by the Italian G. D. Cassini in the early 1670s as the Paris Observatory's first director. Such telescopic discovery was reflected in the painted ceiling decoration of the cosmic Planetary Rooms at Versailles, further manifesting royal interest in the progress of astronomical science which the king also practised himself; and on the ceiling of the Hall of Mirrors by Le Brun, in which the allegorical figure of the king's *Glory* bathed in golden light holds aloft an astrolabe as she drives the king's chariot on.[178]

At Louis' visit to Colbert's establishment of the royal mirror manufactory in April of 1666, the king was reported to be '*incantato*' (under the spell) of the looking glass, whose 'enchantment' he later brought to the gallery at Versailles.[179] The occasion for the king's visit was to view the first mirrors it produced. Though the documentation does not permit certainty, it was likely the king's own suggestion to decorate the arcades of his gallery with the brilliant effects of wall-length reflective mirrors.[180] If Louis' royal imagery was of specular splendour and crystalline brilliance, the Hall of Mirrors was

---

[175] Huygens, 1690; Newton, 1704, who was working on mirrors, optics, and light from the 1660s.
[176] Saule, 2010.   [177] Saule, 2010.   [178] Milovanovic, 2010.
[179] Thuillier, 2007, 31; Bondue, 2010.   [180] Suggested by Milovanovic, 2007, 14.

its fullest manifestation. Here were staged the major state receptions and entertainments of Louis' reign, in a full display of French luxury resplendently redoubled through the lightsome mirror reflection of the arcaded wall. In his early ambassadorial receptions in the Hall of Mirrors, as from the King of Siam in 1686, Louis appeared dressed in a robe of gold-silk encrusted with diamonds, while his gifts comprised rock-crystal mirrors and gilt-edged cast-glass medals of his portrait as miniatures of the gallery's crystalline splendour.[181]

As the Hall of Mirrors neared completion in the 1680s it was the *Mercure Galant* that carried news of its unfolding beauty to readers at home and abroad. Court fashions of interior decoration appeared alongside those of dress à la mode, as the objects and materials of a newly French *luxe*. The disposition of Louis' magnificent silver furnishings for the Hall of Mirrors, no longer extant but known from descriptions in the *Mercure Galant*, included rows of silver-chased orangery vases of 'golden fruit', and caryatid *torchères* along the walls.[182] In a fairy-tale echo of the Hall of Mirrors, the conclusion to Perrault's rendition of *Sleeping Beauty* staged a nuptial banquet in a *salon* of mirrors to the accompaniment of violins and oboes, while d'Aulnoy's *Bluebird* describes a mirror of 2 × 6 leagues in which 60,000 women could admire themselves in a fantastic allegory of the *Galerie*'s great size; just as the castle of Perrault's Bluebeard prince is fitted like a fairy-tale Versailles with tapestries, cabinets, sofas, ornamental tables, and magnificent full-length mirrors framed in silver and gilt.[183] At Versailles, the brilliance of the mirror decoration in the Hall of Mirrors was further enhanced by myriad gilt-chandeliers and wall-sconces of candlelight reflected and magnified in cut-crystal glass pendants, also of an increasing complexity in their prismatic faceting. At night, the mirrors magnificently amplified the gallery's torches and candles with their myriad reflections. During daylight, the mirrors reflected the windowlight from the gardens beyond, amplified by its ornamental pools and fountains. In the words of the Hall of Mirror's inaugural visitors as reported in the *Mercure Galant*: 'This beautiful gallery is like a luminous walkway, lit as if by the sun itself; a July sun is less radiant.'[184]

Forging a decorative order of specular splendour predicated on the brilliance of light redoubled through reflection, the mirrors of the gallery

---

[181] According to Boulenger, 2016, 58. Examples of the glass portrait medallion apparently cast for the occasion include: https://artsandculture.google.com/asset/medallion-with-portrait-of-louis-xiv/EwFhaXpc4UTneg?hl=en (last accessed 2021).

[182] Donneau, 1672–1710, 9 September 1686, 306–8. Arminjon, 2007, offers a sense of what the silver furnishings for the *Galerie* were once like.

[183] Perrault, 1981, 136, 150; d'Aulnoy, 2004, 214.

[184] Scudéry, 1684, 19; Pierre Bourdelot, cited by Saule, 2007, 62.

swept through the subsequent decoration of Versailles, other royal residences, Parisian *hôtels*, and palaces across Europe as the defining materiality of a newly modern interior of specular light reflection, just as the luxury textiles and jewelled dress of Louis' court defined French fashion à la mode. In purloining, and then casting in grand scale the clear and brilliant *cristallo* glass of Murano, Colbert forged a newly modern materiality of light to rival fairy tales. From the plate-glassmakers of the Faubourg St Antoine to the *haute-mondaines* of the Faubourg St Honoré, crystalline was among the pre-eminent materialist signs of Louis' nationalist French political economy of resplendent *luxe*. In taking up the Venetian fairy tales of Straparola, the French *salons* also recast these folkloric narratives of fortune into sparkling social commentary of ready contemporaneous wit. In Perrault, the glass slipper emblematised the glittering fairy tale of Louis' Hall of Mirrors and Colbert's manufactories, the literary mascot of a French economic modernity. Unlike the apparently timeless gems of royal dress and folkloric fairy tales, Perrault, like Colbert, understood glass as a material of the future, whose subsequent history they had instantiated in the modernising methods of the French manufactories. In his substitution of glass for diamond or crystal in the composition of Cinderella's dancing shoe, Perrault epitomised the future of French manufacturing as one that would indeed have a fairy-tale ending. If outshone by Cinderella, as both Perrault and Colbert would have wished, the glassworks of St Gobain remain to this day a pre-eminent French manufacture of a future-facing materiality; while the so-named *Comité Colbert* continues to preside over the trade and export of luxury goods for France.

In the words of the early eighteenth-century Parisian cultural critic, Etienne La Font de Saint-Yenne, Louis XIV's mirror-interior was indeed 'a fairy-tale wonder' composed of an evanescent materiality of light whose cascading reflection represented French modernity: 'Mirrors, in which we see the narrative of their effect like a fairy-tale, and a marvel beyond all belief... for a nation avid for all that is brilliant and new.'[185] As a metonymy of Louis' Hall of Mirrors, Perrault's glass slipper was as real, and as fictional, as a fairy tale or a mirror reflection, just as Anatole France had recognised. In Perrault, the courtier-academician's ever courtly phrase was: 'All cedes to the power of the well-chosen gesture.'[186] His glass slipper emblematised French culture in the age of Louis, which had spun straw into French gold like the fabled queen Pédauque, transforming humble cinders and sand into the princely splendours of the great Hall of Mirrors at Versailles.

---

[185] La Font, 1747, 13, 15.   [186] Perrault, 1690, 11.

References

Aarne, Antti & Stith Thompson (1961) *The Types of the Folktale: A Classification and Bibliography*, Helsinki.

Adams, Tracy (2014) *Christine de Pizan and the Fight for France*, Philadelphia.

Aikema, Bernard (2009) 'La Casta Susanna', in *Jacopo Tintoretto: Actas del congreso internacional Jacopo Tintoretto*, eds. Miguel Falomir & Bernard Aikema, Madrid, 45–9.

Albero, Miguel M. (2016) 'La imagen de la monarquía: Moda, espectáculos y política: Maria Teresa y Margarita Teresa de Austria en busca de un Nuevo Olimpo', *Anales de Historia del Arte*, 26, 103–39.

Alcouffe, Daniel (2001) *Les Gemmes de la Couronne*, Paris.

Allerston, Patricia (1998) 'Wedding Finery in Sixteenth-Century Venice', in *Marriage in Italy 1300–1650*, eds. Kate Lowe & Trevor Dean, Cambridge, 25–40.

Alligo, Pietro (2017) *Tarocchi dal Rinascimento a oggi*, Turin.

Arizzoli-Clémentel Pierre & Pascale Gorguet Ballesteros (2009) *Fastes de Cour et Cérémonies Royales: Le costume de Cour en Europe 1650–1800*, Paris.

Arasse, Daniel (1992) *Le détail: Pour une histoire rapprochée de la peinture*, Paris.

Armeno, Cristoforo (1557) *Pelegrinaggio di tre giovani figliuoli del re di Serendippo*, Venice.

Arminjon, Catherine (2007) *Quand Versailles était meublé d'argent*, Paris.

Armstrong, Edward (1944) 'The Symbolism of the Swan and the Goose', *Folklore*, 55:2, 54–8.

Artephius [pseud.] (1612) *Le secret livre: Les figures hiérogliphiques de Nicolas Flamel*, Paris.

Baddeley, John Frederick (1919) *Russia, Mongolia, China*, 2 vols., New York.

Balzac, Honoré de (1901) *About Catherine de Médicis* (1841), trans. Clara Bell & George Saintsbury, New York.

Basile, Giovan Battista (1891) *Il Pentamerone overo Lo cunto de li cunti* (Naples, 1634), ed. Benedetto Croce, 2 vols., Naples.

Basile, Giovan Battista (1932) *The Pentamerone*, trans. Benedetto Croce, London.

Baskin, Cristelle (1991) 'Griselda, or the Renaissance Bride Stripped Bare by Her Bachelor in Tuscan *Cassone* Painting', *Stanford Italian Review*, 10:2, 153–75.

Bauden, Fréderic & Richard Waller (2020) *Antoine Galland (1646–1715) et son journal: Actes du colloque internationale*, Leuven.

Bayer, Andrea (2008)*Art and Love in Renaissance Italy*, The Metropolitan Museum of Art, New York.

Beasley, Faith (2006) *Salons, History, and the Creation of Seventeenth-Century France: Mastering Memory*, Aldershot.

Benserade, Isaac de (1653) *Ballet Royal de la nuict, divisé en quatre parties, ou quatre veilles, et dansé par sa Majesté le 23 Fevrier 1653*, Paris.

Benserade, Isaac de & Jean-Baptiste Lully (1671) *Psyché* (first performed 1656) Paris.

Bettelheim, Bruno (1975) *The Uses of Enchantment: The Meaning and Importance of Fairy Tales*, New York.

Bimbenet-Privat, Michèle (2009) 'La littérature cosmétologique: traités et secrets de beauté', in *Le bain et le miroir: soins du corps et cosmétiques de l'Antiquité à la Renaissance*, eds. Michèle Bimbenet-Privat & Isabelle Bardiès-Fronty, Paris, 280–97.

Biringuccio, Vanoccio (1540) *De la Pirotechnia*, Venice.

Bloom, Rori (2022) *Making the Marvelous: Marie-Catherine d'Aulnoy, Henriette-Julie de Murat, and the Literary Representation of the Decorative Arts*, Lincoln.

Boodt, Anselm de (1609) *Gemmarum et Lapidum Historia*, Hanover.

Bondue, Didier (2010) 'La guerre des miroirs: Colbert et Murano au regard de deux fonds des Archives d'Etat de Venise (1665–67)', *Revista Arhivelor*, 2, 179–210.

Botley, Paul (2004) *Latin Translation in the Renaissance: The Theory and Practice of Leonardo Bruni, Giannozzo Manetti, and Desiderius Erasmus*, Cambridge.

Bottigheimer, Ruth (2002) *Fairy Godfather: Straparola, Venice, and the Fairy Tale Tradition*, Philadelphia.

Bouchenot-Déchin, Patricia (2018) *Charles Perrault*, Paris.

Boulenger, Jacques (2016) *L'Ameublement français au grand siècle* (1907), London.

Brown, Bill, ed. (2004) *Things*, Chicago.

Burdon, Michael & Jennifer Thorpe (2010) *The Ballet de la nuit: Rothschild B1| 16|6*, New York.

Bycroft, Michael & Sven Dupré, eds. (2019) *Gems in the Early Modern World: Materials, Knowledge, and Global Trade, 1450–1800*, Cham.

Cagnat-Deboeuf, Constance, ed. (2008) *Madame d'Aulnoy's* Contes de fées, Paris.

Canepa, Nancy (1999) *From Court to Forest: Giambattista Basile's* Lo cunto de li cunti *and the Birth of the Literary Fairy Tale*, Detroit.

Carboni, Stefano & David Whitehouse (2001) *Glass of the Sultans*, The Metropolitan Museum of Art, New York.

Carré, Anne-Laure & Sophie Lagabrielle (2019) *Flacons, fioles et fiasques de l'antiquité à nos jours*, Actes du troisième colloque international de l'association Verre & Histoire, Rouen-Vallée de la Bresle, 4–6 April 2013, Paris.

Celenza, Christopher (2018) *The Intellectual World of the Italian Renaissance: Language, Philosophy, and the Search for Meaning*, Cambridge.

Cole, Charles Woolsey (1939) *Colbert and a Century of French Mercantilism*, 2 vols., New York.

Conticelli, Valentina (2007) *Guardaroba di cose rare et preziose: Lo studiolo di Francesco I de' Medici: arte storia e significati*, Lugano.

Cugy, Pascale (2017) *La dynastie Bonnart: peintres, graveurs, et marchands de modes à Paris sous l'Ancien Régime*, Rennes.

D'Ablancourt, Nicolas Perrot (1650) *Les origines de la langue française*, Paris.

Dahlberg, Anne Marie (1996) *Royal Splendour in the Royal Armoury*, Stockholm.

Darnton, Robert (2009) 'Peasants Tell Tales: The Meaning of Mother Goose', in *The Great Cat Massacre and Other Episodes in French Cultural History* (first published 1984), New York, 9–74.

D'Aulnoy, Marie-Catherine (1697) *Contes des fées*, Paris.

D'Aulnoy, Marie-Catherine (2004) *Contes des Fées*, ed. Nadine Jasmin, Paris.

DeJean, Joan (2005) 'Cinderella's Slippers and the King's Boots: Shoes, Boots, and Mules', in *The Essence of Style*, New York, 83–103.

D'Elia, Anthony F. (2004) *The Renaissance of Marriage in Fifteenth-Century Italy*, Cambridge, MA.

Dew, Nicholas (2009) *Orientalism in Louis XIV's France*, Oxford.

Diderot, Denis & Jean le Rond d'Alembert (2002) *La fabrication des glaces* (first published c. 1770), *Encyclopédie Arts & Métiers*, 28 vols., Paris (1761–88), Paris.

Donato d'Eremitana (1624) *Elixir vitae*, Naples.

Donneau de Visé, Jean, ed. (1672–1710) *Mercure Galant*, Paris.

Dooley, Brendan (2016) *Angelica's Book and the World of Reading in Late Renaissance Italy*, New York.

Duggan, Anne (2005) *Salonnières, Furies and Fairies: The Politics of Gender and Cultural Change in Absolutist France*, Newark.

Duggan, Anne (2019) 'The *Querelle des femmes* and Nicolas Boileau's *Satire X*: Going beyond Perrault', *Early Modern French Studies*, 41:2, 144–57.

Dundes, Alan (1983) *Cinderella: A Casebook*, New York.

Eisenstein, Elizabeth (2012) *The Printing Revolution in Early Modern Europe*, Cambridge, UK.

Elias, Cathy Ann (1989) 'Musical Performance in 16th-Century Italian Literature: Straparola's *Le piacevoli notti*', *Early Music*, 17:2, 161–74.

Fagnart, Laure (2016) 'L'Appartement des Bains et le Cabinet des Peintures du Château de Fontainebleau sous le Règne d'Henri IV', in *Henri IV: Art et Pouvoir*, ed. Colette Nativel, Tours, 53–65.

Febvre, Lucien (2009) 'Civilisations matérielles et folklores' (first published 1939) *Vivre l'histoire*, Paris, 818–46.

Ferino-Pagden, Sylvia (2006) 'Pictures of Women, Pictures of Love', in *Bellini, Giorgione, Titian and the Renaissance of Venetian Painting*, eds. David Alan Brown & Sylvia Ferino-Pagden, National Gallery of Art, Washington, DC and Kunsthistorisches Museum, Vienna, 190–235.

Fioravanti, Leonardo (1564) *Specchio di Scientia*, Venice.

Forsyth, Hazel (2013) *The Cheapside Hoard: London's Lost Jewels*, Museum of London, London.

Fortini Brown, Patricia (2004) *Private Lives in Renaissance Venice: Art, Architecture, and the Family*, New Haven.

Fouchard, Gilles (2005) *La mode*, Paris.

Fournier, André Le (1530) *La décoration d'humaine nature et ornement des dames*, Paris.

Fowles, Severin (2010) 'People Without Things', *An Anthropology of Absence: Materializations of Transcendence and Loss*, eds. Mikkel Bille, Frida Hastrup, & Tim Flohr Soerensen, New York, 23–41.

Freedberg David (1997) *Citrus Fruit, Paper Museum of Cassiano dal Pozzo*, Series B, Part I, London.

France, Anatole (1955) 'Dialogue sur les Contes de Fées', in *Le livre de mon ami* (1885), ed. J. Heywood Thomas, Oxford, 140–67.

Galland, Antoine (1704–17). *Les mille et une nuit*, 12 vols., Paris.

Gell, Alfred (1992) 'The Technology of Enchantment and the Enchantment of Technology', in *Anthropology, Art and Aesthetics*, eds. Jeremy Coote & Anthony Shelton, Oxford, 40–66.

Gerritsen, Anne & Giorgio Riello (2015) *The Global Lives of Things: The Material Culture of Connections in the Early Modern World*, New York.

Girouard, Marc (1976) *Hardwick Hall*, London.

Gladstone, William (1858) *Studies on Homer and the Homeric Age*, Oxford.

Goethe, Johann Wolfgang von (1810) *Farbenlehre*, Tübingen.

Goodman Soellner, Elise (1983) 'Poetic Interpretations of the "Lady at her Toilette" Theme in Sixteenth-Century Painting', *The Sixteenth-Century Journal*, 14:4, 426–42.

Gorce, Jérome de la (2009) 'Les ballets du roi', in *Louis XIV L'homme et le roi*, eds. Nicolas Milovanovic & Alexandre Maral, Versailles, 344–47.

Greenhill, Pauline, Jill Terry Rudy, Naomi Hamer, & Lauren Bosc, eds. (2018) *The Routledge Companion to Media and Fairy-Tale Cultures*, New York.

Griffey, Erin, ed. (2019) *Sartorial Politics in Early Modern Europe: Fashioning Women*, Amsterdam.

Grimm, Jacob & Wilhelm Grimm (1857) *Kinder- und Hausmärchen*, Berlin.

Haase, Donald (2010) 'Decolonizing Fairy-Tale Studies', *Marvels & Tales*, 24:1, 17–38.

Hahn, Cynthia & Avinoam Shalem, eds. (2020) *Seeking Transparency: The Medieval Rock Crystals*. Berlin.

Hale, J. R., ed. (1973) *Renaissance Venice*, London.

Hannon, Patricia (1998) *Fabulous Identities: Women's Fairy Tales in Seventeenth-Century France, Amsterdam.*

Harris-Warrick, Rebecca & Carol Marsh (1994) *Musical Theatre at the Court of Louis XIV: Le Mariage de la grosse Cathos*, Cambridge.

Haudicquier De Blancourt, Jean (1697) *De l'art de la verrerie*, Paris.

Havard, Henry (1887) *Dictionnaire de l'ameublement et de la decoration*, 4 vols., Paris.

Heidenreich, Conrad E. & Arthur J. Ray (1976) *The Early Fur Trade: A Study in Cultural Interaction*, Toronto.

Hennard Dutheil de la Rochère, Martine, Gillian Lathey, & Monika Wozniak (2016)*Cinderella across Cultures: New Directions for Research and Interdisciplinary Perspectives*, Detroit.

Hess, Catherine & Karol Wight (2005) *Looking at Glass: A Guide to Terms, Styles, and Techniques*, The J. Paul Getty Museum, Los Angeles.

Hoffmann, Kathryn A. (2016) 'Perrault's 'Cendrillon' among the Glass Tales: Crystal Fantasies and Glassworks in Seventeenth-Century France and Italy', *Cinderella across Cultures: New Directions and Interdisciplinary Perspectives*, eds. Martine Hennard Dutheil de la Rochèree, Gillian Lathey, & Monika Wozniak, Detroit, 52–80.

Horta, Paolo (2017) *Marvellous Thieves: Authors of the Arabian Nights*, Cambridge, MA.

Howell, James (1641) *Epistolae*, London.

Huet, Pierre-Daniel (1683) *De optimo genere interpretandi*, The Hague.

Huygens, Christiaan (1690) *Traité sur la lumière où sont expliquées les causes de ce qui lui arrive dans la réflexion, & dans la refraction et particulièrement dans l'étrange refraction du cristal d'islande*, Leiden.

Jones, Ann Rosalind & Peter Stallybrass (2000), *Renaissance Clothing and the Materials of Memory*, Cambridge.

Jones, Christine A. (2016) *Mother Goose Refigured: A Critical Translation of Charles Perrault's Fairy Tales*, Detroit.

Jones, Jennifer (2004) *Sexing la Mode: Gender, Fashion, and Commercial Culture in Old Regime France*, Oxford.

Jonson, Ben (1853) *The Works of Ben Jonson*, Boston.

King, Margaret (2014) *Venetian Humanism in an Age of Patrician Dominance*, Princeton (1986).

Knothe, Florian (2009) 'Depictions of Glassmaking in Diderot's *Encyclopédie*', *Journal of Glass Studies*, 51, 154–60.

Kraatz, Anne (1989) *Lace: History and Fashion*, London.

Kren, Claudia (2013) *Alchemy in Europe: A Guide to Research*, London.

Kühn, Holger (2015) *Die leibhaftige Münze: Quentin Massys' Goldwäger und die altniederländische Malerei*, Paderborn.

La Font de Saint-Yenne, Etienne (1747) *Réflexions sur quelques causes de l'état présent de la peinture en France avec un examen des principaux ouvrages exposés au Louvre le mois d'août 1746*, Paris.

La Fontaine, Jean de (1668) *Fables*, Paris.

La Fontaine, Jean de (1669) *Amours di Psyché et de Cupidon*, Paris.

La Force, Charlotte-Rose de Caumont de (1697) *Les Contes des Contes*, Paris.

Lampugnani, Agostino (1648) *Della carrozza da nolo, overo, del vestire & usanze alla moda*, Bologna.

Lanaro, Paola (2006) *At the Centre of the Old World: Trade and Manufacturing in Venice and the Venetian Mainland*, Toronto.

Lau, Kimberly (2016) 'Imperial Marvels: Race and the Colonial Imagination in the Fairy Tales of Madame d'Aulnoy', *Narrative Culture*, 3:2, 141–79.

Le Guérer, Annick (2005) *Le parfum, des origines à nos jours*, Paris.

Lett, Matthieu (2020) *René-Antoine Houasse (vers 1645–1710): Peindre pour Louis XIV*, Paris.

L'Héritier de Villandon, Marie-Jeanne (1696) *Oeuvres Meslées, contenant . . . Les enchantements de l'éloquence, Les avantures de Finette*, Paris.

Lieberman, Marcia (1972) 'Some Day My Prince Will Come: Female Acculturation through the Fairy Tale', *College English*, 34, 383–95.

Lüthi, Max (1982) *The European Folktale: Form and Nature* (1947), trans. John D. Niles, Philadelphia.

Magnin, Charles (1852) *Histoire des Marionnettes en Europe depuis l'antiquité jusqu'à nos jours*, Paris.

Magnanini, Suzanne (2008) *Fairy-Tale Science: Monstrous Generation in the Tales of Straparola and Basile*, Toronto.

Mailly, Louis de (1698) *Les Illustres Fées*, Paris.

Makdisi, Saree & Felicity Nussbaum (2008) *The Arabian Nights in Historical Context: Between East and West*, Oxford.

Marin, Louis (1990) 'Préface-Image: Le frontispice des *Contes* de Perrault', *Europe*, 739, 114–22.

Marinelli, Giovanni (1562) *Ornamenti delle leggiadre donne*, Venice.

Marly, Diana de (1987) *Louis XIV and Versailles*, London.

Martin, Marie-Pauline (2015) 'Le Cabinet des Beaux-Arts de Charles Perrault: Le monument d'un moderne', *Revue de l'Art*, 190:4, 9–18.

Milovanovic, Nicolas (2007) 'La Galerie des Glaces: Un décor exemplaire', Nicolas Milovanovic & Alexander Maral, *La Galerie des Glaces: Charles Le Brun maitre d'œuvre*, Paris, 14–19.

Milovanovic, Nicolas (2010) 'Les sciences dans les décors de Versailles', in *Sciences et curiosités à la Cour de Versailles*, ed. Béatrix Saule, Paris, 98–103.

Milovanovic, Nicolas & Alexander Maral (2007) *La Galerie des Glaces: Charles Le Brun maitre d'œuvre*, Paris.

Milovanovic, Nicolas & Alexandre Maral (2009) *Louis XIV: L'Homme and Le Roi*, Paris.

Milovanovic, Nicolas & Nathalie Volle, eds. (2013) *La galerie des glaces après sa restauration: Contexte et restitution*, XXVI Rencontres de l'Ecole du Louvre, June, Paris.

Molà, Luca (2000) *The Silk Industry of Renaissance Venice*, Baltimore.

Molière [Jean-Baptiste Poquelin] (1660) *Les précieuses ridicules* (first performed 1659), Paris.

Montchrétien, Antoine de (1615) *Traicté de l'oeconomie politique*, Rouen.

Motte, Antoine Houdar de la (1697) *L'Europe galante: Ballet en musique representée par L'Academie Royal de Musique*, Paris.

Murat, Henriette-Julie Castelnau de (1698) *Contes de Fées*, Paris.

Neri, Antonio (1612) *L'arte vetraria*, Florence.

Newton, Isaac (1704) *Opticks or a Treatise on the Reflections, Refractions, Inflexions, and Colours of Light*, London.

Nichols, Thomas (1652) *A Lapidary or the History of Pretious Stones*, London.

Nocentini, Serena (2010) 'Specchio delle mie Brame: Segreti di Bellezza al Tempo di Tiziano', in *Donna allo Specchio: Tiziano a Milano*, eds. Valeria Merlini & Daniela Storti, Milan, 121–6.

O'Bryan, Robin (2019) *Games and Game-Playing in European Art and Literature, 16th–17th Centuries*, Amsterdam.

Ó Gráda, Cormac, with Guido Alfani, eds. (2017) *Famine in European History*, Cambridge.

Padiyar, Satish (2020) *Fragonard: Painting Out of Time*, London.

Paresys, Isabelle (2019) 'Dressing the Queen at the French Renaissance Court: Sartorial Politics', in *Sartorial Politics in Early Modern Europe: Fashioning Women*, ed. Erin Griffey, Amsterdam, 57–74.

Pastoureau, Michel (2013) *Vert: Histoire d'une couleur*, Paris.

Pastoureau, Michel & Elisabeth Taburet-Delahaye (2013) *Les secrets de la licorne*, Musée de Cluny, Paris.

Paulicelli, Eugenia (2014) *Writing Fashion in Early Modern Italy: From Sprezzatura to Satire*, Abingdon.

Pearce, Michael (2018) 'The Dolls of Mary Queen of Scots', *Edinburgh Castle Research Reports*, February, 1–52.

Perrault, Charles (1661) *Le miroir d'Orante*, Paris.

Perrault, Charles (1668) *Peinture: Poème*, Paris.

Perrault, Charles (1679) *Labyrinte de Versailles*, Paris.

Perrault, Charles (1688) 'Le siècle de Louis le Grand, Poème', in *Parallèle des Anciens et Modernes*, Paris.

Perrault, Charles (1688–92) *Parallèle des Anciens et Modernes*, 4 vols., Paris.

Perrault, Charles (1690) *Le cabinet des beaux-arts*, Paris.

Perrault, Charles (1694a) *Apologie des femmes*, Paris.

[Perrault, Charles.] (1694b) Préface, *Dictionnaire de l'Académie Françoise*, 2 vols, Paris, I, n.p.

Perrault, Charles (1696) *Les Hommes Illustres*, Paris.

Perrault, Charles (1697) *Contes de ma mère l'Oye*, Paris.

Perrault, Charles (1759) *Mémoires de ma vie* (published posthumously), Paris.

Perrault, Charles (1981) *Contes*, ed. Jean-Pierre Collinet, Paris.

Perrault, Charles (1999) *Contes*, ed. Nathalie Froloff, Paris.

Perrault, Charles (2009) *The Complete Fairy Tales*, trans. Christopher Betts, Oxford.

Porta, Giambattista della (1589) *Magia Naturalis*, Naples.

Prechac, Jean de (1698) *Contes moins contes que les autres*, Paris.

Propp, Vladimir (1968) *The Morphology of the Folktale* (1928), trans. Laurence Scott, Austin.

Pullins, David (2014) 'Techniques of the Body: Viewing the Arts and Métiers of France from the Workshop of Nicolas I and Nicolas II de Larmessin', *Oxford Art Journal*, 37:2, 135–55.

Rameau, Pierre (1725) *Le maître à danser*, Paris.

Reddan, Bronwyn (2016) 'Thinking through Things: Magical Objects, Power, and Agency in French Fairy Tales', *Marvels & Tales*, 30:2, 191–209.

Reed, Gervais (1974) *Claude Barbin, libraire de Paris sous le règne de Louis XIV*, Paris.

Ribeiro, Aileen (1995) *The Art of Dress: Fashion in England and France, 1750–1820*, London & New Haven.

Richards, John F. (2014) *The World Hunt: An Environmental History of the Commodification of Animals*, Berkeley.

Riello, Giorgio & Ulinka Rublack, eds. (2019) *The Right to Dress: Sumptuary Laws in a Global Perspective, c. 1200–1800*, Cambridge.

Robert, Raymonde (1982) *Le conte de fées littéraire en France de la fin du XVIIe à la fin du XVIIIe siècle*, Nancy.

Roche, Daniel (1994) *The Culture of Clothing: Dress and Fashion in the Ancien Regime*, trans. Jean Birrell, Cambridge.

Rosetti, Giovanni Ventura (1548) *Plictho de l'arte de tintori*, Venice.

Rosetti, Giovanni Ventura (1555) *Notandissimi secreti de l'arte profumatoria: A fare ogli, acque, paste, balle, moscardini, uccelletti, paternostri, e tutta l'arte intiera*, Venice.

Rozario, Rebecca-Anne Do (1560) *Fashion in the Fairy Tale Tradition: What Cinderella Wore*, Cham, 2018.

Sabellicus, Marcantonio (1560) *Opera Omnia*, Basel.

Saslow, James (1996) *The Medici Wedding of 1589: Florentine Festival As Theatrum Mundi*, London & New Haven.

Saule, Béatrix (2007) 'La galerie au temps de Louis XIV: de l'ordinaire à l'extraordinaire', in *La Galerie des Glace: Histoire et Restauration*, Dijon, 54–73.

Saule, Béatrix, ed. (2010) *Sciences et curiosités à la Cour de Versailles*, Paris.

Savary, Jacques (1675) *Le parfait negoçiant*, Geneva.

Savary, Jacques (1723 [published posthumously]) *Dictionnaire universel de commerce*, 3 vols., Paris.

Schneider, Jane (1989) 'Rumpelstiltskin's Bargain: Folklore and the Merchant Capitalist Intensification of Linen Manufacture in Early Modern Europe', in *Cloth and Human Experience*, eds. Annette Weiner & Jane Schneider, Washington DC, 177–213.

Scoville, Warren (2008) *Capitalism and French Glassmaking 1640–1789* (first published 1950), Berkeley.

Scudéry, Madeleine de (1684) 'Conversation de la magnificence et de la magnanimité', in *Conversations nouvelles sur divers sujets, dédiées au roi*, Paris, I, 1–118.

Seidel, Linda (1993) *Jan van Eyck's Arnolfini Portrait: Stories of an Icon*. Cambridge.

Seifert, Lewis (2004) 'On Fairy Tales, Subversion, and Ambiguity: Feminist Approaches to Seventeenth-Century *Contes de Fées*', in *Fairy Tales and Feminism: New Approaches*, ed. Donald Haase, Detroit, 53–71.

Semmelhack, Elizabeth (2010) *On a Pedestal: From Renaissance Chopines to Baroque Heels*, Toronto.

Sewell, William (1986) 'Visions of Labour: Illustrations of the Mechanical Arts before, in, and after the *Encyclopédie*', in *Work in France: Representations,*

Meaning, Organization and Practice, eds. Steven Kaplan, Steven Koepp, & Cynthia Koepp, Ithaca & London, 258–86.

Shakespeare, William (1623) *First Folio*, London.

Shawcross, Rebecca (2014) *Shoes: An Illustrated History*, London.

Smith, Bruce (2009) *The Key of Green*, Chicago.

Smith, Pamela H. (2004) *The Body of the Artisan: Art and Experience in the Scientific Revolution*, Chicago.

Spadaccini-Day, Barbara (2009) 'La poupée, premier mannequin de mode', in *Fastes de Cour et Cérémonies Royales: Le costume de cour en Europe 1650–1800*, Pierre Arizzoli-Clémentel & Pascale Gorguet Ballesteros, Paris, 226–9.

Stensen, Niels [Nicolaus Steno] (1669) *De solido intra solidum naturaliter*, Florence.

Straparola, Giovanni Francesco da Caravaggio [pseud.] (1550, 1553) *Le piacevole notti*, 2 vols., Venice.

Straparola, Giovanni Francesco da Caravaggio [pseud.] (1560) *Les Facecieuses Nuictz*, trans. Jean Louveau, Lyon.

Straparola, Giovanni Francesco da Caravaggio [pseud.] (2012) *The Pleasant Nights*, trans. W. G. Waters (first published 1894), ed. Donald Beecher, 2 vols., Toronto.

Straparola, Giovanni Francesco da Caravaggio [pseud.] (2015) *The Pleasant Nights*, trans. and ed. Suzanne Magnanini, Toronto.

Strong, Roy (2002) *Feast: A History of Grand Eating*, London.

Strong, Roy (1966) 'Three Royal Jewels: The Three Brothers, the Mirror of Great Britain, and the Feather', *The Burlington Magazine*, 108:760, 350–3.

Sullivan, Margaret (1994) *Bruegel's Peasants: Art and Audience in the Northern Renaissance*, Cambridge.

Swann Jones, Steven (1995) 'Bibliographic Essay', *The Fairy Tale: The Magic Mirror of the Imagination*, Abingdon, 119–40.

Tatar, Maria (1992) *Off with Their Heads! Fairy Tales and the Culture of Childhood*, Princeton.

Tatar, Maria (2015) *The Cambridge Companion to Fairy-Tales*, Cambridge.

Tavernier, Jean-Baptiste (1676) *Les six voyages de J. B. Tavernier*, 2 vols., Paris.

Teverson, Andrew (2019) *The Fairy Tale World*, London.

Thépaut-Cabasset, Corinne (2017) 'The *Mouche* or Beauty Patch', in *Fashioning the Early Modern*, ed. Evelyn Welch, Oxford, 135–8.

Thépaut-Cabasset, Corinne & Pamela J. Warner (2007–8) 'Présents du Roi: An Archive at the Ministry of Foreign Affairs in Paris', *Studies in the Decorative Arts*, 15:1, 4–18.

Thuillier, Jacques (2007) *La Galerie des Glaces: Histoire et Restauration*, Dijon.

Trivellato, Francesca (2000) *Fondamenta dei vetrai: Lavoro, tecnologia e mercato a Venezia tra sei e settecento*, Rome.

Tyden Jordan, Astrid (1988) *Queen Christina's Coronation Coach*, Stockholm.

Vincent, Monique (2005) *Le Mercure Galant: Présentation de la première revue feminine d'information et de culture, 1672–1710*, Paris.

Voltaire [François-Marie Arouet] (1966) *Le siècle de Louis XIV* (first published 1752), 2 vols., Paris.

Voltaire [François-Marie Arouet], with Jean-Philippe Rameau (1745). *La Princesse de Navarre: Comédie-ballet en trois actes*, Paris.

Vries, Jan de (2003) 'Luxury in the Dutch Golden Age in Theory and Practice', in *Luxury in the Eighteenth Century: Debates, Desires and Delectable Goods*, eds. Maxine Berg & Elizabeth Eger, London, 41–56.

Vries, Jan de (2008) *The Industrious Revolution: Consumer Behaviour and the Household Economy, 1650 to the Present*, Cambridge.

Vries, Jan de (2010) 'The Limits of Globalization in the Early Modern World', *Economic History Review*, 63:3, 710–33.

Warburg, Aby (1999) 'The Theatrical Costumes for the *Intermedi* of 1589' (first published 1895), *The Renewal of Pagan Antiquity*, Los Angeles, 495–546.

Warner, Marina (1994) *From the Beast to the Blonde: Fairy Tales and Their Tellers*, London.

Welch, Evelyn, ed. (2017) *Fashioning the Early Modern: Dress, Textiles, and Innovation in Europe, 1500–1800*, Oxford.

Yates, Frances (1947) *The French Academies of the Sixteenth Century*, London.

Zecchin, Luigi (1987–90) *Vetro e vetrai di Murano*, 3 vols., Venice.

Zipes, Jack, ed. (2001) *The Great Fairy Tale Tradition: From Straparola and Basile to the Brothers Grimm*, New York.

Zuber, Roger (1968) *'Les belles infidèles' et la formation du goût Classique: Perrot d'Ablancourt et Guez de Balzac*, Paris.

Cambridge Elements ⁼

The Renaissance

John Henderson

Birkbeck, University of London, and Wolfson College, University of Cambridge

John Henderson is Professor of Italian Renaissance History at Birkbeck, University of London, and Emeritus Fellow of Wolfson College, University of Cambridge. His recent publications include *Florence Under Siege: Surviving Plague in an Early Modern City* (2019), and *Plague and the City*, edited with Lukas Engelmann and Christos Lynteris (2019), and *Representing Infirmity: Diseased Bodies in Renaissance Italy*, edited with Fredrika Jacobs and Jonathan K. Nelson (2021). He is also the author of *Piety and Charity in Late Medieval Florence* (1994); *The Great Pox: The French Disease in Renaissance Europe*, with Jon Arrizabalaga and Roger French (1997); and *The Renaissance Hospital: Healing the Body and Healing the Soul* (2006).

Jonathan K. Nelson

Syracuse University Florence, and Kennedy School, Harvard University

Jonathan K. Nelson teaches Italian Renaissance Art at Syracuse University Florence and is research associate at the Harvard Kennedy School. His books include *Filippino Lippi* (2004, with Patrizia Zambrano); *Leonardo e la reinvenzione della figura femminile* (2007), *The Patron's Payoff: Conspicuous Commissions in Italian Renaissance Art* (2008, with Richard J. Zeckhauser); and he co-edited *Representing Infirmity. Diseased Bodies in Renaissance Italy* (2021). He co-curated museum exhibitions dedicated to Michelangelo (2002), Botticelli and Filippino (2004), Robert Mapplethorpe (2009), and Marcello Guasti (2019), and two online exhibitions about Bernard Berenson (2012, 2015). Forthcoming publications include a monograph on Filippino (Reaktion Books, 2022) and an Element, *The Risky Business of Renaissance Art.*

Assistant Editor

Sarah McBryde, *Birkbeck, University of London*

Editorial Board

Jane Tylus, *Yale University*
Kate van Orden, *Harvard University*

About the Series

Timely, concise, and authoritative, Elements in the Renaissance showcases cutting-edge scholarship by both new and established academics. Designed to introduce students, researchers, and general readers to key questions in current research, the volumes take multi-disciplinary and transnational approaches to explore the conceptual, material, and cultural frameworks that structured Renaissance experience.

Cambridge Elements [≡]

The Renaissance

Elements in the Series

Paradoxes of Inequality in Renaissance Italy
Samuel K. Cohn, Jr

The World in Dress: Costume Books across Italy, Europe, and the East
Giulia Calvi

Cinderella's Glass Slipper: Towards a Cultural History of Renaissance Materialities
Genevieve Warwick

A full series listing is available at: www.cambridge.org/EREN

Printed in the United States
by Baker & Taylor Publisher Services